THIS SH!T WORKS

A NO-NONSENSE GUIDE TO
NETWORKING YOUR WAY TO MORE
FRIENDS, MORE ADVENTURES, AND
MORE SUCCESS

JULIE BROWN

www.juliebrownbd.com

Cover design: JuLee Brand for designchik.net

This Shit Works / Julie Brown —1st ed.

Paperback ISBN 978-1-7348379-0-2

ebook ISBN 978-1-7348379-1-9

Available in Paperback, eBook, and Kindle

CONTENTS

THIS BOOK IS DEDICATED TO

- **my network**; thanks for contributing to my success and happiness, and allowing me to contribute to yours;

- **Chris** (duh);

- **Julie Uno**; for your constant mentoring, sometimes ass kicking, and that one time in college you totally saved my butt

HOW THIS SHIT HAPPENED AND WHO THIS SHIT IS FOR

Note: While I'm not dropping f-bombs willy-nilly, I do swear when the situation calls for it. Prepare mentally for occasional curse words.

I had already planned on helping my husband launch his own architecture firm. What I hadn't planned on was doing it during the biggest financial crisis since the Great Depression—much of it driven by a crash in the housing market. Timing can be a real bitch.

It was 2010. Half of the architecture and construction industry had been laid off. And those who still had jobs were working at reduced salaries in order to keep as many people employed as possible.

We had been planning for Chris to venture out on his own since 2008. At that time, there had been some chatter about a housing bubble, but no one really understood the dire situation the country would soon be facing.

As his launch date drew nearer, Chris began to rethink the idea. But I knew having his own firm was his dream. I refused to let him postpone making that dream come true. So, on a whim in May of 2010, I packed our car, threw a couple of our special wine club bottles in my bag, and told him we were going away for the weekend.

Chris and I are both baseball fans; so much so that the first condo we purchased together was across the street from Fenway Park, the oldest baseball stadium in the country, and home of the Boston Red Sox. When we purchased the condo in 2003, we had no idea that the very next year the Red Sox would come back from a 3-0 deficit to beat the New York Yankees in the AL East and then go on to win the whole shebang, the entire enchilada, by sweeping the St. Louis Cardinals in four games in the World Series. No longer would the infamous "1918" chorus be sung by our rivals while visiting the historic stadium.

So I pointed the car toward Cooperstown, New York, home of the National Baseball Hall of Fame, where neither of us had been. Cooperstown is a five-hour drive from our home, allowing plenty of time for us to discuss how scary it would be for him to quit his job in this economy, but also how prepared we were for him to do this. Over dinner that night, savoring one of our California wine club bottles, we toasted each other and made it official: He would give his notice on Monday.

I won't lie, it was scary. But in less than a year he was making more money than he had at any of his previous jobs, and he was so much happier. *So much happier.* How did it happen so quickly? I'll tell you how: That very next Monday, as Chris gave his notice, I got to work calling my network. Some of the people I talked with had met Chris before, but some only knew him by name as my husband.

One of the friends that I called that morning was a person who I have traded leads with, traveled to conferences with, co-hosted events with, done just about every business development activity with, and become close friends with. She mentioned that my call could not have come at a better time. She had literally just gotten out of a meeting with a long-time client who needed to have a six bedroom dorm designed and built as a summer slammer project. She needed to put a team together that week. She asked if Chris would be interested.

(Does a bear shit in the woods?)

I said of course he was, and that I'd have Chris call her that day to get started. He hadn't even left his job yet and he already had his first client.

It felt amazing to get that project right out of the gate, but in order to build a practice you need a number of projects and a continuous pipeline of leads, so I continued to make calls.

I phoned another friend of mine who had met Chris at industry parties over the years. I let him know that Chris had officially started his own firm and asked if he knew anyone who might need an architect. He responded that he was on the board of a local private school, that they had a classroom renovation coming up over the summer, and if we were interested he would mention Chris at the next board meeting. Despite the fact that his firm was brand-spanking new and he had to compete against two other well-established firms, Chris was awarded the project partly based on the strength of my relationship with that board member.

I asked the CFO of the architecture firm where I worked if he would talk with Chris about the financial side of running a business. I had bonded with this CFO a while back when I discovered that he was running a marathon in Las Vegas right before I would be running my first marathon in Boston. We became running buddies and even raced together a few times. He agreed to get together with us. At that meeting he handed

Chris the floor plans to his carriage house, which needed a major renovation, and hired him on the spot.

In addition to calling members of my network individually, I began hosting dinner parties at our house every Friday night so that I could introduce the people in and around my network to Chris, his capabilities, and his talents. (This is a tip I got from Keith Ferrazzi's book *Never Eat Alone*.) To this day I can look back at those evenings and trace the beginnings of a number of close friendships, business collaborations, and projects.

Chris' rapid success was due to two things:

1. Of course I'm biased, but he is great at what he does.
2. The power of networking.

That second item is what I am great at—building a web of genuine relationships with people in my industry. Not merely professional relationships, but real, genuine friendships. This ability to build a web of support was so well-honed, in fact, that it empowered me to launch my own company five years later.

I absolutely could not have made these phone calls nor hosted these dinner parties if I hadn't already put the work into building a robust network around me. This book is a guide to get you to the same point. In these pages I'll show you exactly how to build relationships that are rewarding personally and professionally and build a robust network of friends, contacts, and clients.

If you think that you don't have what it takes to build a power network, that you don't have the right personality, the right education, the right connections, I call bullshit. If I've done it, trust me, so can you.

I'M NOT SPECIAL

If there's anyone whose life experience would suggest that they are *not* good at building relationships, it's me. I have struggled my whole life to feel worthy of love and connection. As a kid, I was abandoned by a father whose addiction to heroin was so strong that it left room for little else.

Today we talk about heroin addiction much differently than we did 30 years ago. Now, we have a better understanding of how opioid addiction works and how we need to strip away the stigma of addiction so that we can begin to treat the underlying problem. When I was a kid, heroin addicts were junkies. My dad was a junkie. I was the daughter of a junkie. Being abandoned by your parent because their tether to addiction was stronger than their tether to you, their own flesh and blood, will go a long way toward making you think you aren't deserving of pretty much anything good.

I know everyone has an inner critic—an interior voice that tells you all the reasons why you suck, why you'll never have good things, and why it would be better for everyone involved if you just stayed inside your house and whiled away your life watching bad TV. And while it's not about comparison, I've got to believe that my early experiences cultivated one of the loudest, meanest inner critics of all time, although I know that plenty of people had less than ideal upbringings. Perhaps you're one of them.

To say that I did not have the advantage of being well-connected is an understatement—there was absolutely no one in my orbit to help me get into an Ivy League school, or a pivotal internship, or to give strategic introductions.

What I've learned is that connections to high-powered people are nice-to-haves, but they are not must-haves when it comes to creating a power network that will launch your career forward.

In one of my early jobs, I worked at a small architecture firm where I was just one of a few people who did not attend Harvard. My inner critic tried to convince me—yet again—

that I didn't belong in or deserve that position, and that my pedigree didn't stack up to the rest of the firm. However, I was also the youngest person in the firm to hold a director's position. No one else thought I wasn't cut out for the job.

Your inner critic will do its best to convince you that you can't walk into a networking event and work the room, or that people won't be invested in your success, or that you don't deserve certain relationships, or that you simply aren't cut out for this, or that you don't deserve a high level of success. Your inner critic is an asshole and a liar.

Despite that nasty voice in my head, I went out and created a strong, loving, and supportive network *because I had to.* I knew I couldn't rely on my family to back me up. I also knew how important it is to have a web of people around me because I didn't have one growing up. The positive thing that came out of all this is that I realized that people are inherently good and if you put out good efforts to get to know people, you will receive good efforts in return. I realized that *this shit works.*

All the things I have struggled with in my life have given me the tools I needed to be here, to be present, and to kick ass. That's not to say that I know everything there is to know about networking because I don't. But I am committed to continuing to learn every day.

I built a network strong enough to launch two businesses, and so can you. At any stage of your career you can start putting the pieces together that add up to an amazing, powerful, and generous web of supporters. In this book I share with you all the tips and tricks I have learned in my twenty years as a marketing and business development professional. This book is not the only book you will ever need, but it is definitely one of the important tools in your toolbox for you can use to help create a network that knows you, likes you, trusts you, and is invested in your success.

I'M NOT A MOTIVATIONAL SPEAKER

I hope that this book inspires you, that it motivates you, and that it gives you the tools to create a network around you that allows you to achieve your goals, whatever those goals may be. But let's get one thing straight. I am not a motivational speaker.

I do not like to listen to motivational speakers. Listening to a motivational speaker will inevitably have the opposite effect on me.

Here's an example. I belong to an all-women's real estate networking group. Throughout the year we have a number of informational programs. For the final program of the year the organization always hires a motivational speaker. A couple years ago that speaker was Carey Lohrenz, the first female F14 Tomcat fighter pilot.

In her "motivating" and "engaging" keynote presentation, Carey shared what it was like to work in one of the world's most challenging environments—an aircraft carrier. She went into great detail about what it took to train for this job, what it was like to be dropped into the ocean wearing full aviation gear including a parachute that will inevitably tangle around you, weigh you down, pull you underwater within a matter of seconds, drown you, and kill you. She showed pictures from her graduation, where she was interviewed by Wolf Blitzer, because she had made history by becoming the first female to ever graduate that program. She discussed what it takes to navigate high-stress situations, and become a "high-perform-ing" individual.

At the end of the presentation when the applause died down, my friend Tracey looked at me and said with a wide smile, "That was awesome. Aren't you so pumped now?" I looked at her and replied, "No, I'm not pumped at all. In fact, I feel like a colossal failure. I'm never going to be the first female F14 Tomcat fighter pilot, I'm never going to save my own damn life from a parachute that is drowning me because I had to jump out of a jet, I'm never going to be interviewed by Wolf fucking Blitzer, I'm never going to be the first female anything, and I think it's too late for me to become a 'high-performing individual.'"

Carey's talk had motivated Tracey. It made her feel empowered and happy. It had the exact opposite effect on me. I was demotivated. I left feeling that I was somehow... lacking.

I've had similar experiences with other motivational speakers, like Alison Levine. Alison led the first all-female American expedition to Everest. I absolutely loved listening to her, she was funny and self-deprecating and her story was so very interesting. But I left her talk thinking, "I'll never be able to climb Everest." Now, let me be very clear, I don't have any desire to climb Everest. I have never had any desire to climb Everest. But in listening to her story, I found myself thinking, "Why *don't* you want to climb Everest? Why aren't you challenging yourself, and finally what are you doing with your life that you aren't motivated to take on Everest?"

So, this book is here for anyone who has ever wondered, *What if I'm not smart enough? What if I don't come from the right family? What if I don't have the right personality? What if I don't know what I want to be? What if I don't know where I'm going? What if I don't know what my 'Everest' is?*

This book is for you.

No. Screw that. This book is for all of us. No one gets to a point in their lives where they don't need people anymore. No one has all their shit together all the time. No one. We all need a network, and there will be points in everyone's life when you will need that network more than you could possibly imagine. So let's start building it.

ENOUGH ABOUT ME

Let's talk about you for a minute. This book is for you, even—or especially—if:

- **You feel like you lack a pedigree.** Listen, where you come from, no matter where that is, is not a determining factor on where you are allowed to go. You can achieve whatever your heart desires when you work for it. Your inner critic is not allowed to stop you from fulfilling your potential, and your past is not allowed to determine your future.

- **You identify as an introvert.** Introverts can absolutely be amazing networkers and relationship builders. You do not have to be gregarious, or the life of the party, to have real, genuine conversations with people that can be continued after a networking event. Not to mention that because of your introverted nature, you will most likely be over-prepared for your networking event and ready to absolutely kill it once you start getting involved in conversations (something I will teach you how to do in this book).

- **You think networking is a necessary evil.** Networking is so much more than idle chit chat over bagels and coffee at the local chamber breakfast. It has the power to change your career. It doesn't have to be boring, inconvenient, or a time suck either. Networking is not just about going to events and hoping to connect with people, networking is understanding how to ask for strategic introductions, how to connect people in your sphere of influence, and discovering that networking can happen anywhere—the local coffee shop, the ski lift, the sidelines of your kid's soccer game. Networking is all around us.

- **You're 'too busy' to network.** Well, the first thing is, you don't *find* the time to network, you *make* the time.

Once you realize how much it can advance your career, your success, and your happiness (yes, really!), you will delightedly schedule it in your calendar just like any other important activity. By reading this book, you will also learn to spot serendipitous connections and to understand that any conversation can be a networking opportunity—and those aren't things that need a spot in your calendar.

- **You've been told you need to be "more professional."** Oh, if I had a fucking nickel... I cannot tell you how many times I have gotten the results back from a 360-degree review while working at some bureaucratic, soul-crushing company, where being outspoken, energetic, and extroverted is somehow seen as being unprofessional. Well, they can suck it, because leadership and the ability to teach and influence people can look like a lot of different things. You do not need to be 'buttoned-up' or even particularly impressive in order to be a kickass networker. In fact, the more real you are, the stronger your network will be, so long as you aren't authentically a racist, sexist, and/or homophobic douche bag who thinks you're better than other people. You can 100 percent stay true to your authentic self *and* be wildly successful.
- **You're seeking work-life balance.** There is no pill you can take to achieve work-life balance, and there is no magic spell you can cast to somehow be given more hours in a day. But what you can do is work smarter, not harder, and create a network of people around you who advocate for you, refer you, and are ultimately invested in your success. I aim for a work-life blend, and this becomes so much easier to do when we allow ourselves to take down the wall that so often bifurcates our work self from our "real" self.

- **You want to stand out more in your field or in your company.** It is no longer sufficient to just be good at your job. In order to stand out in a bulging population of people with similar qualifications who are looking for the same job or the same clients, you need people to recommend you to their network. In order to do that, people have to know what you do, they have to like you, and they have to trust you to do a good job. That means that in order to stand out, you need to invest in creating relationships both within and outside your firm.
- **You are in transition, seeking a new job, getting back into the workforce, laid off, or starting your own business.** Change in any form can be scary, and sometimes it can feel isolating. Tapping into and expanding your network before and during these times is critical for success. Having a well-formed, multi-level network will be the difference in getting you to where you want to be.

WHAT YOU'LL GET OUT OF READING THIS BOOK

Here's what I promise to deliver in these pages:

- A new way of thinking about networking
- Confidence in your ability to succeed and a new comfort level regarding who you are and what you have to offer
- Information about *why* networking matters that inspires you to get out there
- Plenty of practical tools and strategies so that you always know *what* to do in any situation
- A roadmap for you to follow to start creating your network

- Permission to network in a more comfortable and authentic way
- A sense of relief knowing that you can just be yourself
- The ability to create natural and rewarding relationships within your business that will lead to increased visibility and opportunities in an overcrowded marketplace, greater financial success, and amazing business relationships

When you invest the time in creating a network around you, achieving success is just plain easier. Think of it like a barn raising. In early American life members of a community were enlisted, unpaid, to assist in the building of their neighbors' barns—each member knowing that the favor would eventually be repaid to them. You too are going to need a lot of helping hands in order for you to achieve success. You aren't going to raise that barn alone, and you will be expected to repay the favor.

There is a proverb that states, "If you want to go fast, go alone. If you want to go far, go together." This book shows you how to go far together.

PRIDE, PARADE, OR DAZZLE: HOW BIG SHOULD YOUR NETWORK BE?

While on safari in South Africa in 2019 celebrating our 15th wedding anniversary (take that, marriage statistics), I was—and still am—completely in awe of the creatures that I was able to see so close up. The big five—elephant, lion, leopard, rhino, and buffalo—get their name from being the most dangerous and deadly animals to approach on foot. In addition we were able to see zebras, giraffes, warthogs, impalas, kudus, monkeys, baboons, hyenas, and many more.

Observing these animals in their natural habitat, I learned a lot of shit. No, seriously I learned a lot about their shit. For example, rhinos will create a communal spot to poo each day. And with each rhino producing about 50 pounds of dung daily, that is one huge communal toilet. Unlike rhinos, elephants poop wherever and whenever they feel like it. Let's just say I was very glad that I was wearing ankle-height boots on our afternoon bush walk. I'm also very happy that all the hippos that I saw were somewhat camouflaged in the river—only their eyes giving away their location—since male hippopotamuses fling their poop by spinning their tails around to impress females and to mark their territory. Talk about a literal shit storm.

While on safari I didn't only learn about poop, I also learned about the structure and organization of the groups of each different type of animal:

- A group of lions is called a *pride*, and usually consists of three male lions and a dozen or so females with their cubs, generally around 40 lions in all.
- A collection of elephants is called a *parade* or a *herd*, and can vary in numbers from eight all the way up to 100. Unlike lions, elephants are matriarchal; each herd is led by an elder female. Elephants, like humans, form special bonds between family members, assist each other with the care of their young, and even mourn the dead.
- A collection of zebras is called a *dazzle*. Now, this is my absolute favorite; you can't help but smile thinking of a line of zebras, strutting their stuff, giving everything in the bush the old "razzle dazzle." Zebras live in family groups of up to 20, but during migrations dazzles can swell to more than 1,000 zebras.
- On the other side of the spectrum is the solitary leopard, which spends almost its entire adult life alone.

Each of these animals forms groups of a size that best suits them, and also assists in their survival.

Naturally, because I am so nuts for networking, even when I was on safari I was thinking about it, wondering, what is the best number for a group of humans? What size herd do we need to ensure that we don't just survive, but that we thrive? Do we ever get to a saturation point, when we know enough people and can stop reaching out to make new connections?

Well, contrary to popular belief (especially my mother's), I am not a know-it-all. I can't tell you how many people you have to know in order to be successful. I think it could possibly be different for everyone. I maintain that quality trumps quantity, but I also believe that the more people you know and build relationships with, the more successful you will be.

Even though there's not one hard and fast number of how big your network should be, there is some research that can guide us. For instance, Dunbar's number.

Robin Dunbar is a British anthropologist and evolutionary psychologist whose studies of non-human primates suggests that there is a limit to the number of stable social relationships that the brain can maintain, and that this limit is tied to the size of the neocortex region of the brain. For non-human primates, the number is about 50. When this baseline is applied to the larger human neocortex, it suggests that the number of stable relationships we as humans can effectively maintain is 150.

But you know what Dunbar's number doesn't take into consideration? Databases, customer relationship management software, and other various platforms that help us maintain and monitor the health of our relationships. His research was conducted in 1992, way the hell before reliable internet, social media platforms, iPhones, and texting. At the time of this research you were still waiting for the beep to leave your voicemail message on someone's answering machine. He had no idea that 20 years later we'd be taking pictures of our meals and posting them online in real time, because everyone is so damn interested in what you had for lunch.

But let's take Dunbar's 150 as a *minimum* number. That doesn't mean that each person in your list of 150 connections has the same status. There are different categories of relationships and each category has a target number of people who should fill that role.

Before we dive into what the categories are, we need to get one thing straight. You'll hear me talk more about this in Chapter 6, but the people in these circles don't have to only be "work friends." I don't believe in work friends; regardless of where you meet someone, they are either your friend, or they're not. Someone doesn't have to be in your field in order to be one of your 150 connections. It only matters that you know, like, and trust each other.

OK, now that I've got that off my chest, let's talk about what these categories are. I actually think of them as circles.

Think of your network as four concentric circles surrounding a single nucleus, which is you. The further a circle is from you, the bigger it is. So you have plenty of room to fit your 150 people. But because you can't talk to 150 people every day, or even every week, you've got to do some thinking about who goes where.

THE FIRST CIRCLE: YOUR TOP 5

The first concentric circle is your Top 5. These are the people who are closest to you. They are your ride or die peeps; they are invested in your success and they push you to be the best you can be.

Ideally, your spouse, partner, or main squeeze is one of your Top 5. Warren Buffet and I agree on something (other than the fact that money is nice to have): that the most successful people have one thing in common, and that is a spouse or partner who is invested in their success. This is critical.

The person you choose to walk through this life with should 100 percent want to see you succeed and be willing to help you do so. There is no room for people in your Top 5 (or any concentric circle around you for that matter) who do not want to see you succeed, or are intimidated by your success. This means that if your success allows you to be the breadwinner for your family, it does not cause an ounce of resentment on your partner's part, or an ounce of superiority on yours.

(This is not to say that you can't be wildly successful if you aren't partnered up with someone. Research suggests that single people are more social, and spend a greater portion of their day staying in touch with friends—two things that will help you fill up each of your concentric circles with ease.)

The remaining four people that round out your Top 5 are your strongest networking connections; the people you rely on for information, strategic introductions, advice, guidance, and more. They elevate your thinking, continuously inspire you to be better, and aid in you doing so. You need to pick these people wisely.

Fostering close relationships over time has been nothing short of career-changing for me. I would not be the successful business owner I am today if I didn't have the collective knowledge of my Top 5 to continually help me achieve more, push me to do better, be my cheerleader, and suggest my services to people in need of my skill set.

It's not a one-way street though; you need to be the kind of person who also does these things for your Top 5. You need to constantly help them be better at their job, either via strategic introductions, industry information, referrals, or a well-timed pep talk.

NEXT UP: THE CIRCLE OF 15

Ideally, there are people in your network who aren't your Top 5, but they are still so important to you that they deserve their own ring just beyond the innermost five. This next ring should be about 15 people. You should feel close to these connections—close enough to feel comfortable reaching out to them for almost anything. They should also know they can ask you for help when they need it. This sounds a lot like a top five, and it is; but the reality is that your interactions with this group are less frequent than your closest five. If you talk to the Top 5 multiple times a week, you likely converse with the folks in your Circle of 15 once a week or, at most, once every other week.

MOVING OUT ANOTHER RING: THE CIRCLE OF 50

Knowledge is power, especially in business. Think about your network. Do you have 50 people you can reach out to for information, to bounce ideas off of, to keep you informed about what is happening in the industry, and to refer you? If your answer is no, don't panic. Using all the things I share in this book will help you fill in all of your circles.

Recently I was in a business development meeting with a client where all the principals at my client's firm were at the table. One principal mentioned that a local university had just advertised a request for architectural proposals. My client mentioned that they had been able to secure a position on one of the architectural teams submitting a proposal, but didn't know what other architects were pursuing the project. I picked up my phone and started texting the architects in my network to see if any of them were pursuing the project, and if they were, if my client's firm could join their team. Within minutes I had responses back. I was then able to schedule a quick call to discuss the project with someone who had responded yes. And you better believe I asked them to include my client on their team.

My client looked at me with big eyes and asked how I was possibly able to do this so quickly. I'll tell you the same thing I told him: I can do this because I have fostered at least 50 robust relationships within my industry.

LAST BUT NOT LEAST: THE CIRCLE OF 100

The final circle is filled with acquaintances—people you've had solid conversations with, you make sure to have a one-on-one check-in with when you're at the same event together, you check in with each other (ideally every three or four months, but sometimes it's every five to six months) to see how each other is doing. This circle may seem so far away from the center that it's insignificant, but there is serious power and opportunity here. A recent study showed that 72 percent of jobs that win awards involve people talking to and collaborating with their outer network. Most job opportunities come from this extended network, so don't forget to stay in touch and nurture the people you know but don't necessarily know well or see all the time—they are links in your chain, just as you are a link in theirs.

I call this the Circle of 100, but it can certainly exceed this number, particularly if you have been working for over a decade. Your outer network grows as you grow in your career; you should always be meeting new people and creating a deep extended network that you can tap into.

Is your outer circle 100 strong, or do you need to make some new connections? Are you putting yourself in situations where you can meet people, get to know them, and add them to your network?

I've said it before and I'll say it again, a network isn't going to build itself or happen by mistake, so get out there and start meeting people.

Do I believe that when you hit the numbers in these four circles of connections that you should stop meeting people? Hell no! I look at these numbers as the minimum number of connections you should have. Managing this many relationships takes diligence and finesse, but it can be done, especially when you use customer relationship management (CRM) software to help you organize your contacts, keep track of your interactions with them, and remind you to reconnect with them every 12 weeks. (See Chapter 3 for my recommendations for CRMs.)

CHAPTER 1 TO-DOS:
TAKE AN OBJECTIVE LOOK AT YOUR NETWORK

You really don't want to guess about how big your network is—it's too important to leave up to chance. So take a minute now to assess your circles.

- **Step 1:** Create a spreadsheet with four columns. The left column is your five closest relationships, the next is your Circle of 15, then the next is your Circle of 50, and the column way to the right is your extended network of 100 relationships (or more). (OR, if you want to use a worksheet that's already been created for you, go to juliebrownbd.com/reallygoodshit and download the workbook I've put together for you—it's got a spot for you to list out your circles, as well as a place to list yourself and a checklist for spiffing up your LinkedIn profile.)
- **Step 2:** Now start listing names in each of the four columns. Go through your LinkedIn connections, CRM, and/or email address book to help you remember how many awesome people you know; be sure to include your family and your friends—they are your network too.

- **Step 3:** Determine which column(s) need the most work. Try to determine when you last interacted with each person in your network.
- **Step 4:** If you feel your network is sorely lacking, don't panic; this book will give you the tools to not only fill those columns, but fill them with amazing, genuine relationships.

YOU ARE AWESOME AND YOU DO AWESOME SHIT

Listen, I love social media as much as the next person, but you can't build relationships with the click of a mouse. There is *no better* way to start developing meaningful relationships than to meet someone in person. I'm going to talk *allllll* about how to kick ass at attending networking events in Chapter 3, but there's something you need to do before you walk into any room of new-to-you people. And that is what you are going to discover—and master—in this chapter.

By the time you're done with this chapter—and you've completed the exercise I'm about to talk you through, which you totally will, *right*?!—you'll be ready to approach anyone at any type of event you may attend and have a fun, meaningful conversation without being creepy and while totally being yourself. You will actually be pumped to go to your next networking event. Or at the very least, curious to try out the knowledge I'm about to share with you and test for yourself whether this shit works or not. (You'll be pleasantly surprised to find out that it does, indeed, work!)

I'm even going to go out on a limb and say that by the end of this chapter, you will be excited to attend your next networking event.

Now, a common complaint I hear from people regarding meeting people at networking events is that they don't have anything to talk about.

<insert buzzer noise>

This is false. You have a shit ton to talk about! Don't believe me? Prepare to realize just how many things you actually have to gab about with other people, and how this realization will help you connect with people you've never met before.

It is a fundamental truth that people will do business with—and refer business to—people they know, like, and trust. But you can't just get to know, like, and trust without some personal connection. People won't know, like, and trust you just because you awkwardly introduced yourself and then stuck a business card in their hands. You connect to people by finding things that you have in common. And you have things in common with way more people than you might think.

Once you find those things, you can talk about them, share experiences and stories about them, ask questions about them… all of which are super-quick ways to start forging a relationship and get you to that pivotal state of "know, like, and trust" with someone you didn't even know before you walked into that event.

And when you find people who know, like, and trust you, you will find ways to support each other, either by doing business together directly, or referring business to each other. Which means learning how to talk to other people won't just make networking events more bearable and, dare I say, fun— it will help you make more money! So let's dive in to how to find those things you have in common.

LIST YOURSELF

Every person on this planet is a three-dimensional, multi-faceted being. So are you. And every one of those facets is an opportunity to bond with someone else. But if you only talk to people about what you do, or what they do, for a living, you are carving out such a narrow sliver of who you are that it doesn't leave a lot of room for connection. Worse yet, you ignore all the interesting and amazing things you probably have in common.

Here's how to stop doing that: Make a list of all the awesome things about yourself—who you are in the world and what you like to do in it.

Go ahead, I'll wait.

I think I know what you might be thinking; something along the lines of, *But Julie, I don't have anything interesting to write down.* Hear me when I say this:

You are more interesting than you give yourself credit for, and you have way more to talk about than you think. Put more plainly, you are awesome, and you do awesome shit.

Keeping this basic truth in mind (that you are awesome and you do awesome shit), write down anything that pops into your head about what you like, or how you spend your time, or how you would describe yourself.

Still coming up blank? Here are a few more prompts: What is an ideal getaway for you? Do you love beach vacations with no agenda, just a tropical drink, a good book, and sand between your toes, or do you love on-the-go vacations perhaps exploring foreign cities?

What issues do you care about—the environment, animal welfare, veteran affairs? Add them to your list.

And let's not be too serious here: Are you a snob (or a fanatic) about anything—wine, food, shoes? Put them on the list too.

What about podcasts, everyone listens to podcasts now; what's your favorite flavor: true crime, business, paranormal, history, sports? There's hardly a person on the planet right now who isn't engrossed in a podcast.

Got a hobby? It could be running, canoeing, welding, crocheting sweaters for chickens, whatever floats your boat. It goes on your list.

Think of listing yourself as increasing the surface area upon which you can connect with people. After all, the more you know about someone the more ways you can connect with them.

MY LIST

To help you see how helpful listing yourself can be, I'm going to share with you my list. Here is what immediately pops into my head when I think about all the things that describe me:

- Wife
- Dog mom (yeah, rescue dogs!)
- Sister (big and little) and daughter, granddaughter, aunt, cousin, goddaughter, niece...
- Marathon runner (Boston three times, baby)
- Wine lover
- Craft beer fanatic
- Tequila enthusiast
- Gardener and beekeeper
- World traveler
- Skier
- Avid podcast listener
- Consumer of 'guilty pleasure' TV shows, i.e. anything on Netflix, Bravo, or MTV

That's the down-and-dirty version of my list that came right off the top of my head. Now, let's dig deeper into that and see how those simple things are in fact much more interesting than they might first appear. Once I do that, I think you'll see for yourself that the stories behind the things on your list can be the building blocks to creating deeper, more authentic connections with people.

WIFE

At the time of this writing I have been married to my husband and best friend for 15 years, and we've been together a total of 19 years. Although we are both in the architecture industry, we didn't meet because of work. I met Chris when I was drunk in a bar. (I was 24.) Does this sound scandalous to you? This is how people met before Match, Tinder, Bumble, and all the other shit you single folks have to deal with now. In my day, you met people in real life, not via swiping right. You traded numbers on a napkin because no one had a cell phone, and then if he liked you, he waited the obligatory three days before calling to ask you out on a date. It was a much simpler time: We didn't deal with online relationship statuses, ghosting, or any of that other malarky. But I digress. (See how there's more to the surface of these things about yourself you just wrote down?)

DOG MOM

In 2010 we rescued Royce, a chocolate Lab/German Short-haired Pointer mix, when he was two years old. He had had a rough go of it those first two years of his life and came to us malnourished and mistreated. He also came to us with an unbelievable desire to please, learn, and love. Because one rescue dog is never enough, in 2018 we added Madeline, a nine-week-old German Shorthaired Pointer, to the family. Royce and Maddie come with us everywhere: to work (where they even have bios on my husband's company website); Vermont (where we spend most of our weekends); every car ride to run errands; and to all of our friends' houses.

If we were allowed to bring dogs to all meetings and networking events we would never need another networking book, ever. Dogs are the greatest icebreaker there is. I have had the most wonderful conversations at networking events with other dog lovers. They are such special things to talk about and we all inevitably pull out our phones to show off pictures of our dogs.

SISTER (BIG AND LITTLE) AND DAUGHTER, GRAND-DAUGHTER, AUNT, COUSIN, GODDAUGHTER, NIECE...

Yes, I am the proverbial middle child, one of three girls. My older sister is three years older than me, and my younger sister is eight years younger than me. The age difference between me and my younger sister is the space between my mom divorcing my biological father and marrying my stepdad. So, I guess my little sister is technically my half sister, but I have never thought of it that way. She's my *sister*; she's not half anything. To be honest, I grew up in a bit of a sorority— there had not been a male born on my mother's side of the family in three generations. My grandmother was one of six girls, my mother one of two, I am one of three, and my older sister had one child, you guessed it, a girl. It wasn't until 2012, when my little sister had her first child, that a boy finally made his way onto the family tree, and just for good measure she had another boy four years later. It doesn't even out the gender balance in the family, but it's a start.

Now, lest you think this sorority was made up of the pearl-necklace-donning, cardigan-wearing, ladies-who-lunch kinda

women, you'd be completely wrong. These were Depression-
era, polio-kicking, "I'll give you something to cry about"
women who don't have time for your bullshit or your feelings.
After growing up in this environment, it's no wonder why
building a career in a male-dominated industry didn't seem
that difficult to me.

MARATHON RUNNER

I run a lot. Like, seven days a week, every week. I started running my senior year in college when I was fat and stressed out.
I remember going to the athletic center at the gym and getting
on the treadmill for the first time. I started running, slowly, I
only made it .25 miles. The next day I went back to the gym
and ran .26 miles. That is how it started: running just a little bit
longer each day than I ran the day before. Eventually it became
something I enjoyed doing.

After college I moved to Brookline, Massachusetts, and
joined a gym around the corner from Beacon Street, the same
Beacon Street that hosts the last few miles of the Boston
Marathon before it takes a right on Hereford and then left on
Boylston to the finish line.

A friend of mine at the gym had run Boston a few times before and asked if I wanted to run with him and his group. That
year I said no. The next year, I said yes. I did my research, found
the best training program for my level of fitness, checked with
my doctor to make sure I was fit enough to run, and set a plan
for how I was going to accomplish this feat. I had doubts about
my ability to finish; when you think about running 26 miles
in a row, it seems impossible, and it is impossible if you don't
have all the tools and training in place.

So, I did run Boston, not just once but three times.

My marathon days may be behind be, but running will
always be the very first thing I do every morning. Running

clears my head, it helps me organize my day, and let's be honest, it allows me extra calories for a couple more beers or glasses of wine at night. And now that we have Royce and Maddie, I have the best running partners ever, except for when Royce has to pee on every single tree, and Maddie chases every squirrel—those runs are a little tough.

WINE LOVER

I grew up in an Irish family, predominantly raised by my grandmother who would boil every dinner to within an inch of its life and whose idea of wine was a jug of Carlo Rossi (you know, the one with the handle) that she would keep on the porch all year round no matter the temperature. Suffice it to say I wasn't exposed to good wine or wine culture growing up.

Especially for a person like me, wine can be intimidating. However, the more you learn about and explore the world of wine, the more fun it becomes. Now, wine to me is about traveling to vineyards to understand how it's made, enjoying a bottle (or two) while relaxing with friends, and slowing down the pace at which we travel through this hectic life.

But it wasn't always this way. I had to work really hard to become a wine lover (I know—tough job, right?). For our first anniversary Chris and I planned a trip to California. We started in San Francisco, spent a day in Napa and Sonoma, and then headed up the Pacific Coast Highway to Sea Ranch. Having lived in Italy for a year, Chris was a big fan of red wine, and he thoroughly enjoyed the time we spent at each of the vineyards we visited. My love of wine came more slowly, but it did come, albeit with a lot of practice. And now, Chris and I have traveled all over the United States and afar to visit wineries and taste wine. We've been to Napa, Sonoma, Lodi, Paso Robles, Monterey, Carmel, Santa Barbara, Los Olivos, Willamette Valley, Woodinville, Yakima, Prosser, Walla Walla, even the Hungarian wine festival in Budapest, and most recently, Franschhoek and Stellenbosch, South Africa. Wine travel has become part of the fabric of our marriage. We love sharing the bottles we bring home from our trips with friends, family, and clients.

CRAFT BEER FANATIC

If it wasn't my grandmother drinking Carlo Rossi, it was my mom enjoying Old Milwaukee, so you can see the level of investment my family put into their libations. Needless to say, I wasn't a beer fan to begin with either. In 2004 Chris and I bought a vacation house in Warren, Vermont, which is about a 30-minute drive from Waterbury, Vermont, where the original Alchemist Brewery was located. Beer lovers do not have to be told, but for everyone else, Alchemist is the brewery that produces Heady Topper, once named the best beer in the world. Other Vermont breweries are no slouches, either, including Magic Hat, Hill Farmstead, Long Trail, Von Trapp, Good Measure, and Lawson's Finest Liquids, just to name a few. When we started spending most weekends in Vermont, I began my beer exploration. Now, I love me a good porter or stout after a long day of skiing.

TEQUILA ENTHUSIAST

A couple years ago I went on a no-carb diet. It was terrible. I'll never do it again. But, something semi-awesome came out of that little experiment: I learned that tequila has no carbs and that it is like, OMG, so amazing. When not thrown back as a shot followed by a suck of lime tequila is actually super tasty sipped, on the rocks with some fresh lime juice. I will never forgive bars that serve over-sugary, sonic-lime-green margaritas—tequila, you deserve better. Did I mention no carbs?

GARDENER AND BEEKEEPER

I don't want to be a farmer, but I love the idea of a backyard filled with flowers, herbs, and vegetables. To be able to walk out the screen door from the kitchen, into the garden, and pick something fresh to incorporate into dinner just feels right. Sharing your bumper crops with neighbors and canning your produce on hot summer days so you can open them and enjoy them on cold winter nights also feels right. Drying your own herbs so you know they aren't filled with pesticides, that feels right too. Which brings me to the bees. Four years ago I decided to purchase a hive from Best Bees Company, which is a full-service beekeeping operation whose profits fund research to improve bee health. If you haven't heard, bees are in serious fucking danger; decimated by Colony Collapse Disorder in the mid-2000s, bees remain under assault from pesticides, climate change, mites, and habitat destruction. Without bees, crops fail. Without crops, there is no food. Without food—you see where I'm going with this. So not one to sit idly by, I decided to house 40,000 Italian honey bees in my backyard. It's a win-win: They get a safe, pesticide-free environment, filled with pollinator favorites, and I get honey, pounds and pounds of liquid gold every year that I share with neighbors, friends, and clients.

WORLD TRAVELER

My family didn't travel. There were no family vacations to Disney World. My entire childhood was contained in the radius of a two-hour car drive. I didn't take my first flight until I was 17. I had a friend who lived in California so I flew there by myself to look at UCSB for college. I don't think I got on a plane again until I was 19 or 20, when my then-boyfriend's family took me with them on their family trip to Disney World.

When I met Chris four years later, and listened to his stories about living in Rome and traveling around Europe, I was officially jealous and my desire for travel and exploration was ignited. In traveling to all these wonderful places I realized just how insular and isolated my life had been up to that point. I understood the power that traveling has to open your eyes, awareness, and heart to other people, cultures, and customs. I believe that traveling makes you a better person, period.

I forgot to mention the food. Food just tastes better when you are on vacation, probably because you actually have the time to chew and enjoy it. I remember being in Rome and trying filleti di baccala, the deliciously battered and deep fried fillets of salt cod, for the first time. Or when we visited Paris and I ate banana and Nutella crepes for breakfast every morning from the street cart around the corner from our hotel. Or the time we were in Vienna and ate dinner at a small cafe and I had the best apple strudel I have ever eaten in my life.

This is why I can't wear a two-piece bathing suit, folks.

SKIER

This is a story to convince you that you are never too old to learn something new, even if that new thing is jamming your feet into immovable vice grips and strapping long, slippery death sticks to your feet. (I'm not making this sound good, am I?) Once I learned how to do it, skiing became so very fun, but trying to learn how to ski when you are almost 40 is difficult and frustrating and will make you cry in your goggles where you hope no one sees. You will most definitely hate every child on the mountain who whizzes by you with their low center of gravity and their fearlessness, but if you take the lessons and you practice you will get better and you will have fun. My goal for my first ski season was to ski a black diamond before the end of the season. Mission accomplished: I was skiing blacks and trying my hand at moguls by March. I was terrible at them—I pretty much bounced the entire way down—but I was doing them. Now, heading into each new ski season I set new goals, like improving my form, getting faster in the trees, connecting more moguls together, and looking better in my ski pants.

If there is something that you want to learn how to do and have been putting it off, stop making excuses. If you don't start this year you will be at least one year older when you do start, and believe me, it doesn't get any easier as you get older.

AVID PODCAST LISTENER

I am obsessed with true crime. I listen to so many true crime podcasts: *Crime Junkie, True Crime Obsessed, Dr. Death, The Drop Out.* Can you believe there is even a true crime podcast that mixes in wine? It's literally called *Wine and Crime*.

I also listen to history podcasts—*What You Missed In History Class* is my absolute favorite, but Dan Carlin's *Hardcore History* is good too—and I'll listen to anything that has to do with Tudor England.

I'm embarrassed to admit it, but I also listen to a host of ghost-related and paranormal podcasts, but you're not getting any more out of me about that.

GUILTY-PLEASURE TV WATCHER

I work a lot, but I don't work 24/7. I do actually leave time for sleeping, exercise, and my guilty pleasure, watching Netflix and reality TV. Now, lest you judge me too quickly, I only watch reality TV during the doldrums of winter when it's far too dark, icy, and cold to run outside, and I have to run on the treadmill in my home gym. My rule is I don't network on Monday nights—after years of networking I've learned that networking on Monday nights can make me tired throughout the rest of the week. So, Monday nights are my Netflix nights, and because of this, I'm relatively caught up on all of the good shows that everyone is watching and talking about. This has helped me in many networking situations, I've definitely bonded with people over a mutual love of *Peaky Blinders, Stranger Things,* and *Ozark.*

And voila; that's my list. I have been using this simple little tool at networking events and one-on-one business meetings for years. It has connected me to so many people and opened doors that would have otherwise been closed. I have gone on wine-tasting vacations with people I met through networking. I have put together business ski trips to create bonds and memories among the people in my network. I get emails from people I met at events telling me what new amazing podcast I have to listen to, or what new show on Netflix is a must-see. I've even received lists of rare tequilas I have been encouraged to try and find.

Now, you might be thinking, well, vacations and ski trips sound great but what about getting business? Most of these relationships translate into business in one way or another, either directly or by referral. Because the people in my network really know me, like me, and trust me, and because we share so many things in common and are fostering a relationship, they want to see me succeed. This shit works!

FLESHING OUT YOUR LIST OF AWESOME SHIT

Now let's go back to your simple little list of things you are and do, and build it out with interesting stories and more insight on why those are the things you thought about when I asked you to "list yourself." This will make it easier for you to create a conversation around each thing. You can always add new points to your list that you can elaborate on later—you're not set in stone, and neither is your list.

Perhaps you started with the fact that you are a mother, brother, wife, or something to do with your familial connections. What is the story of how you met your partner? If you have siblings think about birth order and whether or not you think it has any effect on personality, occupation, etc.

Did you list how you spend your free time with a hobby? How did you get into this hobby or hobbies? What do you love about it? Is there anything else that you want to learn how to do?

If you listed travel, make a list of all the places you have been on vacation, and try to remember a story from each of those vacations.

For any issues you care about that you wrote down, think about why and how you became so interested in that particular thing.

For the things you love (or are a snob about), try to articulate why they are important to you.

Your list will always be who you are and one of the most powerful tools you have to connect with other people. Your list will also change over time, as the things that interest you in your 20s might not matter that much in your 30s, 40s, and beyond. That's the beauty of the list; it can grow and shrink and morph to be an exhibit of who you are at any point in your life.

Because I believe in the power of listing yourself so strongly, I've created a nicely designed template to help make it easier and more fun—it's part of a workbook I created for you that makes the exercises I share in this book that much easier to do. You can go download it for yourself at juliebrownbd.com/reallygoodshit. (Go ahead, I'll wait.)

If you still need convincing on the power of the "List Yourself" exercise, read a few of the messages I've received from folks who have attended one of my speeches and have been using the "List Yourself" approach when meeting new people:

- *"I was in a virtual networking event yesterday, and my cat jumped onto my lap as my video went live. So I started with,*

'Hi, I'm M and I'm a cat mom.' Everyone laughed. I continued with my list items: 'I'm a Boston College fan, a Doug Flutie fan, and Boston-based. After they got to know me, I let them know that I sell batteries. The first person to comment explained that she too is a cat mom and then most of the conversation revolved around cats. I got two contacts out of the event who will be great referrals for battery sales."

- "I definitely fall into the 'I'm boring, there's nothing special about me' crowd. After writing my list I can now see all my potential conversation topics written right in front of me."

- "I left your workshop and immediately starting writing my list. It's funny how going through that exercise I remembered so many things that I hadn't thought about in years."

- "Going through the 'List Yourself' exercise made me remember who I am at the core, not just what I do for a living."

Listing yourself doesn't just make networking easier, it makes it more fun, more fulfilling, *and* more lucrative, because it helps people know, like, and trust you. Don't just take my word for it—go do it now!

CHAPTER 2 TO-DOS:
LIST YOURSELF

1. Create your list of awesome shit—write down anything and everything that comes to mind.

2. Expand upon that list. If you are an avid book reader, list your top 10 books. If you are a world traveler, list your top five places that you have visited.

3. Think of a story for each of your list items.

4. Create a bucket list of things that you want to experience.

5. The next time you meet someone new, increase the surface area you have available for connection by finding a way to work in some of the things from your list into your conversation.

LEARN HOW TO ROCK A NETWORKING EVENT

If you love attending networking events raise your hand. Did your hand stay firmly gripped to the sides of this book? Thought so. Most people tell me they like going to networking events about as much as they like getting a tooth filled. Which is to say, they hate it.

Networking events can get a bad rap; some people think they are awkward, boring, maybe even a waste of time. That couldn't be further from the truth. Especially now that you've taken the time to list yourself, and you've created so many more ways for you to connect with other people.

In order to get the most out of networking you need to do some research on what events are available to you, and from those events, determine which you should be attending. Whatever industry you are in, I can guarantee there is no lack of networking opportunities for you to choose from almost every day. If you are a new lawyer, look into your local bar association as well as any local young professionals' groups. If you are a small-business banker, check out your local Chamber of Commerce in addition to other professional networking associations. The best thing you can do is to be where your potential clients are, so take a moment to look at your existing and past client list and determine where those types of companies and individuals network. Having a strategy around the ideal rooms for you to be networking in will help you organize your networking time and put the gas pedal down on your success.

If you already like going to networking events, great! But if you hate networking events, tough titty. You *have* to start attending them because they are an integral part of the business development strategy for any business person, no matter how big or small your company is or what industry you are in. You have to embrace the fact that you need to attend events for your business, whether those events are networking events, charity events, awards, or virtual events due to a global pandemic, whatever. Because attending events is absolutely vital to creating a network of lasting relationships.

Yes, you do have to make an effort to get to them, which is often not easy because they generally happen before or after work hours. But with rock-solid networking tips and a plan for each event, you will soon see how important these events are to your career and your business.

Whether you're a lover or a hater, by the end of this chapter you're going to be pumped about going to your next event because you're going to have a new understanding of why attending events matters (hint: it's about so much more than putting in face time or enjoying the passed appetizers); you're going to have a game plan for making the most of them; and you're going to have some simple tools in your back pocket that will help you network like a mofo and have fun while you make important, fulfilling, and potentially lucrative connections. Sounds good, right?

Let's start with something nice and easy: comparing net-working events to something you already know how to do and actually enjoy doing.

NETWORKING EVENTS ARE LIKE BARS—AND THAT'S A GOOD THING

You already know I met my husband in a bar. But you don't know that I've also met some of my very best friends in bars as well. Yep, we walked in as strangers and walked out as friends. So long as you are authentic, it's not cheesy. No one will think you're weird or awkward or a swinger if you're real with them, and genuinely interested in who they are.

Take Jeff and Sue, whom I met at a bar in Vermont.

In my first conversation with these two, I mentioned that my husband Chris and I were going to climb Camel's Hump the next morning with our dog Royce. They said they were also planning on doing the very same hike the next day and suggested we all do it together. Now, to someone else that may sound like a terrible idea, like, *What if these people are crazy, and want to take us into the woods and kill us and use our skin for a blanket?* To which I say, please don't think like that, be-cause the likelihood of that being the scenario is the same likelihood of you winning the lottery—it's most likely never going to happen. Speaking of winning the lottery, we all went on the hike together the next day, and from that day forward we have been the best of friends. Not only do we spend al-most every weekend in Vermont together, but we have also traveled to Steamboat Springs, Telluride, Savannah, Martha's Vineyard, and Val d'Isere together. Our friends have become their friends and I can hardly remember a time when we didn't know each other. All because we started chatting over beers—Schlitz of all things, if you can imagine that. In the craft beer capital of New England, of all places!

Why am I telling you this story, and how does it relate to networking? Because networking events are like bars—they're both a bunch of strangers in a room, having a drink, hoping to not look awkward, and hoping to meet someone interesting to talk to. In fact, many networking events are at a bar or have a bar.

Do you get nervous walking into a bar or restaurant? Probably not. So you shouldn't feel nervous walking into a networking event either.

BEFORE YOU GO

OK, I hear you, you actually *do* feel nervous walking into a networking event. That's just because you haven't learned how to prepare for one yet. (They really should teach this stuff in schools—oh wait, that might put me out of a job. Keep studying calculus, kids!) Let's fix that now, shall we?

DO SOME RESEARCH

I understand that walking into an event blindly without any idea of who you might bump into or meet can be anxiety-producing. Luckily there's a simple way around that: Give yourself the benefit of having information about who is likely to be in the room. How? Do some research.

An easy way to do this is to email the organizers of the event and ask if you can have access to the attendee list. Some organizations will give this information to you freely; others will not. If you are given access to the list, simply take a look at who is attending, see if you know anyone, and reach out to let them know you will be attending as well. That kind of reach-out looks like an email that says something like this:

Hey Joe, I saw that you are registered for the upcoming awards event on Thursday. I am heading there as well. This is my first time attending. Have you attended before? Would you want to meet up before the event, catch up, and then head over together?

This email serves multiple purposes:

- You have now reached out to someone you might not have talked to in a while and reestablished your connection with them.
- You also now have someone you can walk into the event with to help ease any anxiety you might have about walking alone into a room of people.

If you scan the list and you don't know anyone you can still get an understanding of who will be attending and look up some of the folks on LinkedIn. Look at their headshots and see what their role is within their company. If you have time, you can do a simple Google search to find out more about the people who'll be there.

If you don't have access to the registration list, don't panic; with a little bit of sleuthing you can discover a lot of helpful information. Take a look at the event website and see who is sponsoring the event. In general, if a company is sponsoring an event, a number of people from the company will be in attendance. Second, do an Internet search of the event with the previous year's date to see if you can find any pictures. This way you might be able to see a few images with captions and find out who was there the year before.

If you can't find any information as to who will be in attendance, it's OK, as I've got several more tips and tricks to share that will help you approach strangers and start having amazing conversations—even when you don't know anyone.

SET A GOAL FOR THE EVENT

I have excellent news for you. Are you ready? Here it is: You do not have to be at a networking event from start to finish in order for it to be a worthy use of your time. Trust me, I love networking, and I don't have time to stay for the duration of every event I attend. We are all pressed for time.

The secret to making an event a successful endeavor is to set a goal for the time you are able to attend. A great goal would be to meet two new people, or to reconnect with someone in your network that you haven't talked to in a while. That way, as soon as you have accomplished your goal, you have full permission to get out of Dodge. You can customize your goal for each event based on who you expect to be there and how much time you have available.

Setting a goal makes you more effective *and* more efficient—an excellent combination.

REVIEW YOUR LIST

If it sounds like I'm beating a dead horse, it's because I am. Your list is powerful and will help you make so many connections. Take a moment to simply re-read your list so that you know all of the cool things that you are allowed to talk about.

BE AUTHENTICALLY CURIOUS

I want you to be authentically curious when you enter an event. I want you to want to meet new people and learn about them. If you approach each event with an air of curiosity it will help alleviate some of the anxiety you might feel about entering a room of mostly strangers. Everyone in that room has some amazing or interesting story on their list. I want you to discover that about them.

ON YOUR WAY

OK, you've done your research, you've set yourself a goal, you've reviewed your list, and you're authentically curious. You're still not quite ready to bust through those doors and start having more success via networking. There are some basic housekeeping things we should go over before heading into an event, because most people don't spend enough time thinking about and executing on these little gems.

DON'T DRIVE LIKE AN ASSHOLE

If you are going to a networking event where you have to drive to the event, please, for the love of God, do not flip anyone off as you are driving. This becomes more important the closer you get to the event. The last thing you want is to double bird someone and then have them pull up beside you in the parking lot. This will never end well.

MAKE A THOUGHTFUL ENTRANCE

When entering (and exiting, for that matter) business development functions, always hold the door open for the person behind you. You would not believe how many people fail at this most basic act of courtesy. Call me crazy, but I think you can tell a lot about people from the small things they do or do not do. You can bet your ass that if I am walking into a networking event behind you, and you don't hold the door for me, I will say, "Oh, thank you," as if you had held the door for me, just so you feel like shit. Alternatively, when I hold the door for someone and they don't say thank you, I always say, "You're welcome." This is generally met with an immediate, "Oh, sorry, thank you." We learned this in grade school, people: You say please and thank you, and you hold the door for the person behind you. I know you can do this, don't be so self-absorbed that you are incapable of noticing the people around you.

KEEP IT CLEAN

You *have* to check your teeth before entering a networking event. In fact, here's a power tip: Avoid the poppy seed bagels at the buffet table, lest you have everyone focus on the little black spots in between your teeth instead of on your conversation.

Same goes for bats in the cave (aka boogers). Check for 'em! I was at a conference cocktail party once and a gentleman who I have known for years came up to me to say hi and he had the biggest, I mean seriously the *biggest*, booger in his nose. And what was even worse was that every time he breathed through his right nostril it moved back and forth a little bit, waving at me. Now, this was a terrible situation for both of us, for me because I had to tell him about said bat, and for him because it's a bit embarrassing. Don't put yourself or other people in this situation.

On a related note, everyone likes fresh breath. You should make sure that yours is minty fresh. However, this does not mean that you are allowed to chew gum. No one, I repeat, no one likes to look at someone chewing gum like a cow, so, get rid of it before you enter the room.

OK, no boogers in your nose or spinach in your teeth, and you've got fresh breath and you've held the door for the person behind you and thanked the person in front of you. You are ready to start mingling.

CHECK YOUR HANDSHAKE

Wait. Before you start mingling I need to know that you don't have a shitty handshake. Your handshake is your first impression, and 100 percent sets the stage for the rest of your interaction with someone new. Let's go over the rules of a proper handshake.

There are four things that your handshake needs to be:
1. Firm
2. Dry
3. Solid
4. No more than three seconds

Types of handshakes you should never, ever do:
1. **The dead fish**. Nothing says "I don't put any effort into anything" more than a limp handshake. If you cannot muster the energy to give a proper firm handshake I'm pretty sure you can't muster the energy in business either. There is simply no excuse for this type of handshake.
2. **The sweaty palm.** Sometimes you're nervous in networking or meeting situations, but this still does not give you the excuse to make someone else feel uncomfortable because you've wrapped your moist palm around theirs. People will absolutely remember that you made their hand feel icky, so if you are prone to sweaty hands, please make sure you have a cocktail napkin in your hand to absorb any sweat, and shift that napkin to your other hand just before shaking hands. There are always cocktail napkins at networking events; it won't seem weird that you have one in your hand.
3. **The wrestler.** Firm does not mean WWF smackdown. Firm means putting effort into the handshake, not that you want to challenge the other person on the mat, so be conscious of how hard you shake hands. An aggressive handshake is just that—aggressive—and there is no place for that kind of attitude in networking.

4. **The claw (aka the queen).** You are never, under any circumstances, to only offer the tips of your fingers in a handshake (unless you are actually the queen). This type of handshake is downright disrespectful. Give them your whole hand.

ONCE YOU ARE THERE

OK, you are prepared to head to the event now: You've got your list, checked your appearance, and you have an amazing handshake. Let's do this.

SCAN THE REGISTRATION TABLE

When entering a networking event, if there is a registration desk where you need to pick up a name tag, spend a minute or two looking at the names and companies of the other people who will be attending. There may be people attending whom you already know or are friends with, or perhaps a person you have been trying to connect with is registered and this will be your opportunity to finally meet them face to face. Take note of who else will be attending so you can look for them later.

APPROACH PEOPLE

Most people don't have a strongly honed ability to easily approach strangers in work or social settings. But it is a skill, and an important one at that, so there is no time like the present to start developing it. There's no way around it: In order to meet new people and expand your network, you're going to need to introduce yourself to lots of people.

The biggest fear that people have when it comes to introducing themselves to a person they don't know is the fear that the other person will not want to talk to them—otherwise known as rejection. Let's toss that fear aside, shall we? Especially if you are at a networking event, because the entire purpose of people showing up to that event is to meet new people!

Another fear people have is that they will find themselves without anything to say and won't be able to sustain a conversation. This is another thing you can toss right in the shitter because you've done your homework on this. You have your list of awesome shit, and thus you have a large number of topics you can bring up to help get the other person talking.

The easiest way to approach someone you don't know is to walk up to them when they are talking to someone you *do* know. How? Easy: Scan the room for someone you know, and if they are talking to someone you don't know ask if you can join their conversation.

There is a concept in social network theory called *triadic closure*, which states that if two people who don't know each other share a common connection, they will bond more quickly when they meet via this connection. It's similar to the "friends of my friends are my friends" idea.

What if you can't find someone you know? Look for a person who is standing by themselves. I call these people ones because they are not coupled up in a conversation with someone. Aside from meeting someone via a mutual connection, ones are the easiest people to walk up to at an event, because they are usually so grateful that someone is talking to them and has rescued them from standing alone and feeling awkward. Simply go up to the person, introduce yourself using that fantastic handshake of yours, and make their day. This will make both of you feel better about being at the event and networking in general.

When you can't spot someone you know, and the ones all seem to have been scooped up by someone else, you need to start looking around at the groups of people talking to one another to determine which conversations are open and which are closed. Here's how you can tell: If two people are facing each other straight on while talking, they are a closed two. This duo most likely knows each other, and the conversation is just between them.

If you see two people speaking to each other and their bodies are at an outward angle to each other, this is an open two. Open twos are easy to walk up to; their body language is actually inviting other people into the conversation. The same strategy goes for groups of three—look to see if it's a closed three or an open three.

The easiest way to remember the closed versus open idea is to think of a bagel versus a croissant (a brilliant concept I learned from Robbie Samuels' book *Croissants Vs. Bagels: Strategic, Effective & Inclusive Networking at Conferences*). Open twos and threes will look like croissants with an opening in the group of people. A closed two or three will look like a bagel—closed all around the perimeter with the hole in the middle. If it's a croissant you have a free pass to walk in and ask if you can join the conversation.

Another great networking tip is to be open to and be welcoming of others joining in on your conversation. Create openness in your two- and three-person conversations and invite others to join in. In other words, be a croissant!

DON'T BE A DOUCHE

You are not allowed to assess a person's value to you based on their title or the company on their name tag. You are not allowed to be dismissive of the people you meet at events because you believe that they "can't do anything for you" or "aren't important enough" to invest time talking to them. I feel like I shouldn't have to write this, but I do, because I see this shit happen all the time. It even happened to me recently.

I was at a holiday networking event for a local industry group that my husband spends a fair amount of time with. I attended as his guest, but registered under my own company name. We arrived together and began to mingle. There was an open three, Chris knew one of the people, so we approached to say hi. We've established that Chris is an architect; two of the people in this particular open three were builders, the other provided materials to architects and builders. This person, the one who provides materials to architects and builders for their projects, could not have cared less about meeting me. My name tag simply said, Julie Brown, JB|BD. I could tell almost immediately that she thought her networking time was not well spent with JB|BD because she didn't engage in the conversation, and turned her back and exited out of the circle as soon as she could, without even the hint of a "nice to meet you."

Total douche move. Not to mention shortsighted. In her dismissal of me because she didn't think I was worth her networking time, she missed the opportunity not just to be a decent human being, but to also learn how integrated in Chris' business I am, and that because my network brings in about 85 percent of the projects he works on, I also have a major say in what consultants and materials providers he chooses (really, we choose) to work with.

Her immediate and knee-jerk assessment of the value of building a relationship with me could not have been more wrong. Please don't do this. When you meet someone for the first time and you dismiss them because you don't believe they can help you right away, you are looking at it backwards. Your job is to meet people, get to know them, and learn how you can be a good networking partner.

KNOW WHEN TO HIT THE BAR

At certain events, there are just too many people for you to try and analyze open versus closed groups, or sometimes it may seem that they are all closed. When I find myself in a situation like this the first thing I do if it is a night event (or a really fun morning event) is find the line for the bar, and not just because I like me an adult beverage or two. When I am in the line for the bar I know that for a set amount of time, there will be a person in front of me and a person behind me, and I can use this opportunity to introduce myself to either (or both) of them and start a conversation. I also know that I have the entire time I am standing in line to talk with them, and then there is a natural cut off point if I want or need to exit the conversation.

After I leave the bar I scan the room to locate a cocktail table that isn't completely full but also isn't empty. When I find a table that has people, but also has some space for me to put my drink down, I walk up to it and ask if they would mind if I used their table to put my drink down. Viola, I am now at a table with two or three people I don't know and I have every reason to introduce myself and join in on their conversation. I call it the table gap, and it's a great networking trick.

REMEMBER NAMES

Dale Carnegie, author of the self-help classic *How to Win Friends and Influence People*, said, "A person's name is to that person the sweetest, most important sound in any language." Think about that for a second. When you see someone for the second time, or third time even, and they remember your name, I bet it makes you feel special. I bet it makes you feel that your previous interaction meant something to them or made an impression. That's because it did. So, you need to start remembering the names of people you meet.

Here are some tips to help you remember.

1. **Don't get caught up waiting to say your own name; you already know your name.** It will come out naturally. Listen to what the other person is saying instead of anticipating saying your own name. If you don't this is how it will play out: The person will introduce themselves (you won't be listening), you will say, "Hi, I'm Sarah," and then your brain will immediately start freaking out because it now realizes that it has absolutely no fucking clue what the other person's name is. This is when it gets worse, because instead of listening to them talk your brain is consumed with trying to figure out the name that it didn't hear.

2. **So, you heard their name right, now repeat their name before you say your own.** This helps you make sure that you have heard it correctly, and also gives your brain an opportunity to process it. People totally appreciate that you want to make sure that you got their name correct, especially if their name could easily be gotten wrong. For example, a name like Julie might be heard as Julia, or Diane as Diana, Steve as Steven. It makes people feel special when you take the time to make sure you heard their name right.

3. **Make a name association.** Think of something their name rhymes with, or think of a person, famous or otherwise, who has the same name as them. For example, the bane of my existence is that when someone finds out my name is Julie Brown, they immediately equate it with early MTV vjay Downtown Julie Brown. This is my cross to bear, but hey, it works. I once met a man whose name was Budd, so in my mind his name became "Budd with a double D!" That's easy peasy to remember—there was no way I was forgetting that. I once met

a man whose name was Laith. I knew I wasn't going to make a name association with that, so I asked if it was a family name—he replied that his parents were "hippies" and wanted to name him Love and Faith so they meshed it together and came up with Laith. I'll definitely never forget that. We also found out in the course of our conversation that we share the same birthday.

4. **Lastly, use their name.** You don't have to go cuckoo crazy with it, but say their name at least once during your conversation and once again when you are ending the conversation. It will help cement the name in your mind.

With these tools you may not remember every single person's name, but it will make it a lot easier to remember most of them. Don't believe me? Check out this note I received from a workshop attendee.

"I am so happy to tell you that I used your naming convention this week. I started a new job and I'm the only woman, which I'm used to, but it's always hard for me to remember names. I was able to meet and remember 12 new team members, including 'Brian the Biker' and 'Marky Mark Mustache.' Thank you!!!"

ELEVATE YOUR CONVERSATIONS

I have never enjoyed the typical networking banter: "What do you do?" and, "How long have you been at your company?" Blah fucking blah.

Skipping the small talk and allowing yourself to have real, genuine conversations with people is what will set you apart from others at networking events. All it takes to be able to do that is to ask the right questions.

It has been proven that there are certain questions that elicit a dopamine response in the brain. Dopamine is a neurotransmitter that contributes to feelings of pleasure and satisfaction. Let me tell you, if you want to have a pleasantly memorable conversation, dopamine is your best friend.

But you won't get it from typical conversation starters like, "What do you do?" and, "How are you?" The dopamine response to these questions is minimal. Author of *The Science of People*, Vanessa Van Edwards suggests asking questions that she calls sparkers—things that make the other person think about the exciting things in their lives. Possibilities include:

- "Are you working on any exciting projects lately?"
- "What is the highlight of your day so far?"
- "Working on any passion projects?"
- "Any vacations planned?"
- "What was your favorite vacation or trip?"
- "Do you have a hobby or play a sport?"
- "What are you watching on Netflix?"
- "Have you read any good books lately?"
- "What podcasts do you listen to?"
- "Do you have a bucket list?"
- "What is your next big adventure, trip, or goal?"

I absolutely love asking these questions because they are more dopamine producing. They give your brain a little high as it thinks about the answer.

In one of my speeches, I play part of Kalina Silverman's TED talk titled "How to Skip the Small Talk and Connect With Anyone," where she introduces the idea of big talk.

If you haven't watched this TED talk, where have you been? Over five million people have watched it. The talk came out of a social experiment and video series Kalina did while she was studying broadcast journalism at Northwestern University. When Kalina first arrived at Northwestern she was constantly meeting new people, but still felt disconnected, in part due to the superficiality of the conversation she was having with new contacts. It was then that she decided to start skipping the small talk and immediately she started to make more meaningful connections with her peers.

In her TED talk she poses the question:

"What if, when talking to our friends, co-workers, or even complete strangers, we could skip the small talk, and instead talk about things that really matter in life?"

After showing her talk to my audience I challenged each of them to incorporate big talk into an upcoming work or networking event. One participant reached out to me a few weeks later and told me that she hosted a dinner at a conference and used my big talk idea as the ice breaker for the participants. She asked each person around the table to introduce themselves and then tell the other guests one thing about themselves that they probably didn't know. This opened up amazing conversations: One person had sung at Carnegie Hall, one person had met the Pope, and another was a classically trained violinist, another had recently published a book. All these amazing facts came out that would have otherwise gone unknown.

When I ask someone to tell me about their most favorite trip I can see something light up in them as they think back to a cherished experience. I love bringing people back to that place. When someone shares with me what their favorite trip location was, it gives me ideas for my own list of must-visit places, or maybe I've been to the same place and presto! We have that trip in common and can compare what we loved about the location and now we are sharing cherished memories together.

One month, over the course of a few networking events, I had three separate people tell me that Barcelona was their absolute favorite vacation. I had never been to Barcelona, and at that time Chris and I had been trying to figure out where we were going to go for our eighth anniversary. With these three glowing recommendations we decided to go to Barcelona that year. It was amazing, one of my top 10 experiences as far as travel goes. Not only did I get a fabulous experience out of my networking question, it offered me the opportunity to follow up multiple times with each person who had recommended the trip to me. I created lasting relationships with each of these people. I still talk to each of them about travel. One of them also hired the company I was working for, providing much needed revenue at the time. That's the power of big talk.

Crafting questions that are designed to elicit big talk—either from the list I just mentioned or from the list you made about yourself back in Chapter 1—will help you create these dopamine-inducing conversations with people. These are the kinds of conversations that lead to people wanting to know more about you, what you do for a living, how they can stay connected with you, and how they can work with you. It all stems from asking the right questions.

There's only one caveat when it comes to big talk: Before exiting one of these conversations, take a moment to shake everyone's hand again, say how great it was to meet them, let them know that you are looking forward to connecting again, and that you will email them tomorrow. Which leads me to my next point.

AFTER THE EVENT IS OVER

Now that the event is over, the real networking can begin. It's all well and good to go to events, meet great people, and have amazing conversations, but if it ends there, what was the use? If you don't have the discipline and a system for following up with the people you meet, you might as well just stay home and watch *Ray Donovan* in your pajamas. You have to continue to move these relationships along, otherwise the people you meet will forever live outside of your parade, pride, dazzle, or whatever size your network is.

HAVE A SYSTEM TO ORGANIZE YOUR CONTACTS

With all of these amazing dopamine-inducing conversations that you are having, people are inevitably going to ask you what you do and want to exchange business cards with you. Once you get their card, I want you to take a moment to write on the card the date, the event, and a couple things that you talked about. This will make it easier for you to follow up the next day. One vital tool for business development and organizing your network, as I mentioned earlier, is to invest in a customer relationship management (CRM) software or platform. Having a CRM will give you a central place to organize all of your contacts and the data associated with them, including correspondence, meetings, and upcoming appointments or reminders to reconnect. There are a number of CRM options for you to consider, from large, robust platforms like Salesforce, Netsuite and Deltek to more economical options like Pipedrive, Hubspot, Monday.com, and Insightly.

I encourage each person to create a personal CRM database for themselves. I advise this to ensure that no matter where you are, should you change jobs or suffer a layoff, you never lose ownership of your network connections and the historical data associated with each contact. I've seen this happen to far too many people, and I don't want it to happen to you.

FOLLOW UP LIKE A CHAMP

After you meet someone at an event, the follow-up afterward is 100 percent your job and should be done within 24 hours. If you want to ensure that you are building and furthering your relationships and standing out against your competition, you need to take on this responsibility. Most people suck at following up, which is why you need to take the helm in regards to this. Otherwise you are just putting effort, time, and money into meeting people who will never become part of your network.

One of the biggest complaints I hear from people is that they don't know how to follow up after a networking event, or don't know what to say when they are following up. The best way to make sure a conversation can be continued is to ask leading questions of the other person so that they can talk about themselves. People love to talk about themselves, and the more they talk, the more you get to learn about them. The more you know about them, the more things you have to discuss when you follow up, which is why those dopamine-inducing questions are so important.

Below is an example of a follow-up email (that was also copied to my CRM) that I sent after a recent morning networking event where I met two lovely ladies and we got to talking about vacations (I was leaving for Jamaica the next morning!).

Ladies,

It was so nice meeting you this morning at the real estate event. It's always nice to find other women to talk to at these predominantly male events.

S- thank you so much for the tips on Sandals St. Lucia—I'm hoping our next trip is either there or Barbados, although my husband was eyeing Grenada recently as well.

I hope we have an opportunity to see each other again soon. When I am back from Jamaica I will send along potential dates for us to grab coffee and reconnect.

Cheers,

JB

Within 15 minutes of sending this, I received the following back:

Hi J & S,

Yes, it was great speaking with you both. I enjoyed learning about you and your firms. Julie, have a great trip—vacation for us all!!!

I hope to see the two of you at other networking events and, if the opportunity presents itself, to even work together on projects.

Best,

M

And

J & M,

It was a pleasure to meet you both as well! The few connections I made today made me realize I need to attend these events more often. If I hear of any other good events coming up I'll let you know.

Regards,

S

Now, this is where so many people falter. You've sent your email and have gotten a response—great! But now you need to *send another email* to determine how you can create actionable next steps to further the relationship. Remember this is your job; don't assume the other person will initiate the next step. Like I said, most people won't and that's why they don't have a kick-ass network like you're going to have.

Going back to my exchange with S and M (wait, is that weird that I just said that!?), there were a number of ways I could re-engage with them; one simple way would be to send an email upon my return from vacation, letting them both know that I am back and would love to get together for coffee and offering dates and times for them to choose from. A second avenue would be to see what other interesting events are coming up in Boston that both of them might be interested in and email them a link to the event, let them know I thought they might be interested in the event, and ask if they are planning to attend, and if so, if we could meet up ahead of time and go together.

Some of your connections will take longer to respond than my new friends S and M (there I go again) did. Try to not take it personally when someone does not respond to your email immediately or even remotely close to the date you sent it. Life happens every day and people get sidetracked. Remember, they just aren't as good at follow up as you are.

Here is an example of an email exchange that I had with a woman whom I met at a networking event in Seattle. Turns out we were both from the Boston area, and we discovered in our dopamine-inducing, big-talk conversation that we both skied at the same Vermont ski mountain every year, Sugarbush.

Monday July 22, 2019

K,

It was so great meeting you at the cocktail party at XYZ Conference on Monday night.

I am sorry for my delay in sending you an email, but I was only home for a hot minute before I had to get on a plane and fly to Indiana. I'm finally home and catching up on emails.

I would love to get together for coffee or lunch or whatever and talk about what you are working on and of course Sugarbush... Could you send me some dates that work for you between now and the end of August?

Looking forward to it.
Cheers,
JB

Crickets for months. And yes, I totally should have pinged her again, but I forgot to put the action item into my CRM, so I didn't get the prompt to check in with her if I didn't hear back within two weeks. It can happen, even to the best of us, (this is why using a CRM to remind you to reach back out is so important). But, four months later I received this email.

October 16, 2019

Julie,
Wow—I just found a half-written email to you in my drafts from July; therefore, apologies in advance for the very delayed response!

Would love to grab coffee or lunch at some point this fall! My schedule frees up after next week—we are in the midst of fall senior leadership meetings with lots of new leadership so it has been a crazy few months. :)
K.

This interaction proves a couple of points, the first being just because you don't immediately hear back from someone, it does not mean that they are not interested in meeting you. They may have, as happened in this case, gotten sidetracked. The second is that it is never too late to reach out to follow up or reconnect. If you dropped the ball, go back and pick it up. Late is always better than never. Too often people think that they can't reach out to someone because too much time has passed. Who made that rule? Do you know? No? Well then that rule doesn't exist. It's never too late to work on that connection.

PUTTING ALL THE PIECES TOGETHER

In May of 2019 I attended a full-day industry event—morning and afternoon speaker sessions were followed by a cocktail networking event. I strategically chose this event, I did my research, and I knew that this event would give me the opportunity to meet and network with people in the industry that I had not yet been introduced to. (Even someone who has been networking for two decades has people she still wants to meet.) I decided that my goal for the event would be to introduce myself to two new people and start getting to know them.

One of the women that I decided to introduce myself to was the business development director for a construction firm that I knew of, but had not had the opportunity to meet with. We got to talking, and in the midst of asking interesting questions discovered that we had a mutual friend. She had gone to high school and was still close friends with a friend of mine that I met through networking more than a decade ago. So, we of course took a selfie together and texted it to our mutual friend with the caption, "Small world, look who I just met." Our triadic closure—the fact that we shared a mutual friend—had done its job and accelerated our affinity for each other. We talked for a while longer and discussed more fun and interesting things, including how we might be able to work together in the future. After the event we grabbed another glass of wine together, traded business cards, and decided to grab lunch within the next couple weeks.

At our lunch we saved the shop talk for the end, until after we had caught up on our dopamine-inducing questions and learned more about each other. Then we talked about work. She let me know how her firm determined which architects to refer to clients, and I discussed how we determine which builders are the best fit for each of our projects. As a next step, we determined that Chris should visit their office and meet their team. A few weeks after Chris met their team, we got a call from them asking us to partner on a new house for one of their clients.

To recap, this is how it all came together, and what I did to ensure success:

1. I knew what room to be in.
2. I did my research before attending.
3. I had a goal for the event.
4. I used dopamine-inducing questions.
5. I took advantage of triadic closures and mutual connections.
6. I followed up within 24 hours to set the action item.
7. I used our lunch together to learn more about her and her business and how we could work together.
8. I sent a thank-you card after our lunch together (even though I paid).
9. I followed through on my promise to set up a meeting with Chris and her team.
10. We respected their schedule and didn't move our meeting once it was set.

These steps don't just work for me: I recently received an email from a woman who had attended one of my networking presentations who wanted to let me know how my tips had given her the courage to introduce herself to a person she admired and had longed to meet.

Julie,

I adored the seminar you presented. And it was so timely for me. On Thursday morning I arrived early to reserve my front row seat, and HW (speaker) was already there. I went over and said good morning and introduced myself.

I asked if he would like a quick tour of some of my favorite showrooms and he was thrilled. As we traveled the design center we spoke about LA, his latest vacation (thank you for telling me to ask that question), and then he asked me what passion I had besides interior design and I was able to tell him that I had an art exhibit in the brand new FDO showroom. He said, "Let's go see it!"

He studied my work and was complimentary but he also gave me some outstanding ideas on how to monetize it. AND, during his presentation, he mentioned me as his friend and asked everyone to go see my work and purchase one for their clients and themselves!

Had I not taken your advice and studied up the night before and felt confident enough to engage with him I never would have gotten so much attention from him at the event.

Thank you, I hope we can collaborate in the future and if there is anything I may do for you please let me know.
Best,
P

This is just one such story I hear over and over again about how these tips not only work, but help make networking interesting, fun, and rewarding.

CHAPTER 3 TO-DOS:
BE PREPARED

1. Research the organizations and events available to you to determine the best event for you.

2. See if you can get an attendee list and reach out to people in advance of the event.

3. Create goals for each event.

4. Be authentically curious, give a great handshake, and remember those names.

5. Use your "list" to create dopamine-inducing conversations.

6. Follow up! Follow up! Follow up!

CONFERENCE LIKE A BADASS
(It's Not Just About Tchotchkes and Booth Babes)

Conferences are an important piece of your business development strategy. Better yet, they are a ton of fun. I enjoy them for a number of reasons, not the least of which is that conferences generally take place in really fun destination cities, like New Orleans, Nashville, Washington DC, Vegas, and Los Angeles. I've even been to a conference in Honolulu—not a bad locale for a work trip!

Sharing experiences in these fun locations with your co-workers, contemporaries, consultants, and clients is also a slam-dunk for building relationships. I have developed a tight-knit group of friends all because we attend the same conferences every year.

In the weeks leading up to each conference, there is always a flurry of emails that discuss who is coming when, when we can all get together, what touristy things can we do together in our free time, who's planning a dinner on what night, and who is bringing wine for the hotel room pre-game.

They have become my conference family; we've been there for each other during weddings, divorces, births, deaths, medical scares, job losses, the ups and the downs...And yes, we all do business with each other. And that's the other huge reason to attend conferences—they help you make more money.

Conferences are a fantastic way to meet potential clients, referral sources, or lifelong friends...*if* you approach them the correct way.

HOW NOT TO PREPARE

Everyone is always told to prepare an elevator pitch before going to a conference. Do you even know where the term "elevator pitch" came from? In *The New Elevator Pitch* by Chris Westfall I learned that the term comes from old Hollywood, when a screenwriter would wait in the lobby of the studio to catch an unsuspecting executive as he (you know it was always men back then) stepped into the elevator. Then, with the executive trapped in that tiny, moving space, the screenwriter would try to sell his idea (and, yeah, the screenwriters were pretty much all men too) to the decision maker in the 30, 60, or 120 seconds he had before the elevator stopped at the exec's floor.

Sweet baby Jesus that sounds terrible for everyone in that elevator.

Having an elevator pitch isn't inherently *bad*—it can certainly be helpful for you to think about how you explain who you are and what you're about in a succinct way. But you really don't want to lead with it. Why? Because spewing an elevator pitch at another person is a really weird way of communicating. It forces your listener to be completely passive. And, when you start spewing it within seconds of meeting someone, you really have no idea if the other person even gives a rat's ass about what you do.

Assuming that someone wants to know what you do, before they know even a little bit about you, before they have determined if they like you and could potentially trust you, is a big assumption.

That is not to say that you should not be prepared for the inevitable "What do you do question?" when you meet someone new, but you should allow this question to come naturally within the flow of a human-centric conversation. A person cannot refer you to others if they don't know what you do or the services you provide. The optimal platform for you to explain what it is that you do is when they are actually interested and listening. *That's* when you can hit 'em with your little mini talk about what you do.

So, what does that little talk sound like? Well, what it doesn't sound like is an apology, ever. Whatever you do, at whatever stage of your career you are in, have confidence in the importance of your work. I never want you to start off describing what you do with the word "just." I hear things like this all the time: "I'm just an assistant manager;" "I'm just an office assistant;" "I'm just out of school." I am removing the word "just" from your vocabulary. It's one of the few four letter words that I won't allow you to use going forward!

Now that I've gotten that off my chest...Having read somewhere that the human attention span hovers around 11 seconds, which is literally less than that of a goldfish, it would serve you best to keep it short and interesting. The typical elevator pitch of 30 seconds or more is useless; you are simply going to lose your listener along the way. Remember we are not in an elevator, the conversations that we are engaging in at these events, and in our subsequent follow-up, are going to ensure that we end up on a long-distance field trip with the people we meet. I suggest that you pretend that you are limited to 140 characters (or thereabouts, like Twitter) to explain what it is that you do.

There will be ample time later to really explain what it is that you do, the problems you solve, and how you can work together down the road. For now, have a quick, enthusiastic answer for what it is that you do. You can always improvise based on the situation you are in. For me I could say something as simple as, "I love connecting people. I work with companies to streamline their growth strategies by teaching them how to be better relationship builders." Or if I am talking about the professional speaking side of my business I could say, "I am a professional speaker. I love speaking about the power of networking and relationship building. I'll actually be speaking at (insert next event here)."

These examples are short and to the point, but to get to that point, you can't get bogged down in a big, longwinded explanation of everything your job entails. It's got to be fairly quick so that you can get right into having interesting, dopamine-inducing conversations (which we talked about in Chapter 3); the kinds of conversations that lead the other person to want to learn more about you and then ask you what you do for a living.

GETTING THE MOST BANG FOR YOUR BUCK

Conferences generally take place over a number of days, and more often than not require some form of travel. The investment to attend a conference is usually a four-figure investment by the time you register, get a hotel room, book transportation, and cover your meals and entertainment costs.

I want you to get past the money factor and the fact that it will take you away from your office for a few days.

Whether you are attending a conference in the hopes of creating connections that you can convert to clients, or whether you are attending for your own personal career development, this will be time well spent.

Now, given the time and financial commitment of attending conferences you should make sure that you are doing everything you can to get the most out of your time there. Lucky for you, I've got 11 tips that will make attending conferences more fun, more effective, and much more likely to lead to more business. I've used these tips to grow my own business. I've also shared them with folks I have coached, and they too have gotten great results.

11 TIPS TO GET THE MOST OUT OF ANY CONFERENCE

1. Make sure that you are staying at the same hotel as everyone else. Why? A tremendous amount of networking will take place in the elevators, the lobby, the breakfast restaurant, and the hotel bar. *You want in on this action.* Missing it will cost you a lot more than the $40 you might save by staying across the street. A companion to this tip is to book your room far enough in advance that you can be sure that you'll be staying at the conference hotel.

2. Prior to the conference, look at the attendee list to see if there are any clients, prospects, or others from your network attending that you want to connect with while you are there. Reach out to them in advance to let them know you are attending as well, and that you hope you'll have an opportunity to connect while you are both there.

3. Reach out to your network in advance to see who else might be going, and suggest that you travel together. I always do this, whether it's driving together or booking the same flight. So much networking and

relationship building can be done in cars, on trains, and in airports. Travel time is part of your conference time. Don't let it go to waste.

4. When you arrive at your destination, take a quick walk to the nearest drugstore to purchase some water and some Gatorade. All that conferencing, networking, and schmoozing will leave you parched; you are going to want plenty of water and electrolytes on hand so that you can stay hydrated and energized. Grab some Advil too; just saying.

5. While at the conference, it can be tempting to go back to your room to check emails after the main panels are over. But you want to attend all of the networking events and cocktail parties. Remember why you are here: to connect with new people. So unless those new people are somehow partying in your room you aren't going to meet them there.

6. Host your own event that doesn't compete with the conference agenda. For example, invite a select group of clients and prospects to a dinner that follows the conference happy hour or cocktail party. This way, you get more focused time with a small group of people without missing out on the opportunity to meet new people. I like to make my dinner reservation for a big enough number that I can invite one or two people I meet at the conference to join us.

7. Don't just be a barfly—actually attend the sessions of the conference. Being able to talk to other attendees about what you have learned shows that you are interested in gaining knowledge. It will also provide you with additional talking points and timely conversation starters.

8. If you are attending a session because you would like to meet the speaker, don't wait until after their presentation when everyone else is trying to get face time with them. Instead, get to the session room 15 minutes early and approach the speaker prior to their talk, telling them how interested you are in hearing them speak. As a public and keynote speaker myself, I can attest to how well this works.

9. Bring enough business cards with you so that you never run out and are never without one when someone asks for your card.

10. If you have invested in a booth, which is generally a large financial investment, do not stand at your booth looking at your phone the entire time. I cannot tell you the number of conferences I have attended where I have walked through the exhibit hall and seen booths that were either empty or manned by someone who was engrossed in their phone the entire time. Make it a rule that whenever you are at your booth your phone is out of sight. This will allow you to focus your attention outward and actually *work your booth*. Meaning, say hi to the people walking by, create an inviting atmosphere, and make it easy for people to approach your booth and ask you questions about your firm or product.

11. Give yourself plenty of time to follow up with the people you meet at the conference. It makes no sense to invest the time and money in attending conferences if you don't have a plan for follow up. You need to schedule the time in your calendar either for when you are traveling home or in your office the next morning. This ensures that you follow up in a timely manner while everything is fresh in their mind. Believe me,

if you do not follow up within 24 to 48 hours, it won't happen. Your normal business activities will take over, the conference will be a blur, and when you finally have the time to reach out to follow up, you'll think that it's been too long and you won't do it.

HOW A ONE-HOUR CAR RIDE LED TO SIX FIGURES OF INCOME

One of the women in my network is an owner's project manager. She helps her clients navigate through their design and construction projects, facilitating the selection of architects, consultants, and builders, all while keeping the project on schedule and within budget.

When the two of us met we immediately bonded over our love of travel. Twice I have booked adventures based on her recommendation—once to Barcelona and the second time to Zambia to see Victoria Falls. We make sure to connect over coffee at least twice a year to discuss where we are in our businesses and to catch up on our travels.

At our latest coffee date she told me the story of a conference she had recently attended, one that, with my advice, she had approached in a completely different way.

The conference was in Boston, about an hour drive for her. So the first thing she did was reach out to one of her contacts to see if he was attending the conference. When he said he was, she suggested they meet up ahead of time and drive to the conference together. He mentioned that he was already hitching a ride with someone else, and suggested that she join them.

Now, this is where she would have normally backed out of the idea of carpooling, wondering if she really wanted to be in a car for an hour with someone she had never met. But she wanted to test out my advice and try a new approach to attending conferences. So she said yes.

Over the course of that one-hour car ride, they all talked about what they do, why they were attending the conference, and life in general. Because she had spent that time in the car with them she didn't have to go into the conference alone; she had two people as her wingmen, ready to introduce her to more people. The conference felt friendlier and easier to navigate.

About six months later, the friend of the man who also rode in the car that day—the woman my friend didn't know before the conference, and might never have met if she hadn't forced herself to try something new—called her to say, "I think you do what I need." It just so happened that this person sat on the board of a nonprofit that was in the beginning stages of its first building project. On this woman's recommendation, my friend was awarded the project, even though the architect had suggested a different owner's project manager.

While my friend was working on this project, another member of that nonprofit's board asked if she would be the owner's project manager for another nonprofit where this person was also on the board. It actually wasn't just one project—it turned out to be three separate projects.

Through that project, my friend got referred to yet another project. That simple act of reaching out in advance and connecting over commuting time has led to five projects, resulting in consulting fees in the six figures, and will no doubt lead to even more.

I have gotten a tremendous amount of work via the connections and relationships that I have fostered at conferences. For example, in 2010—a tough time for architects since the construction market had totally imploded—I was selected to put together a team to design a $10 million project without having to go through any kind of the normal bidding processes. I was awarded this project by the vice president of operations of a local academic institution whom I met at one of the conferences I regularly attend. Now here's the thing: I met him at the hotel bar. (Remember my tip about making sure you book early enough to get a room at the conference hotel?) This story is a perfect example of why you absolutely want to take advantage of all the serendipitous meetings that will happen at that particular hotel.

When we met, we hit it off immediately. I learned that his campus was an hour and a half from Boston, so I made plans to come and tour the campus with him once we got back from the conference. Over the course of a year, I visited him a few times. A few months after my last visit, he called me to tell me that the school had just received a $10 million donation, and that the president wanted to build a new hockey and basketball rink. He asked if I could put a team together to meet with him the next day. My response was, "Is the Pope Catholic? Of course I can put a team together. Thank you for thinking of me."

I need to reiterate that this was a time when every firm needed work, and were slashing their fees in order to win any project they could get their hands on. Because of my relationship with this key decision maker, not only did my firm not have to compete against any other firm, but they also didn't have to reduce their fees or spend valuable funds on the proposal and interview process.

THE CONFERENCE BOND

The great thing about conferences is that they bring different people from all over the place to convene together for the same purpose. Sometimes that alone can catapult the know, like, and trust factor.

During that conference I attended in Hawaii that I mentioned at the start of this chapter, I randomly met someone who would go on to become a very important friend to me during a difficult time. Well, actually, it wasn't random at all—I was following the tips I've shared in this chapter. That is how well they work.

Because the conference was in Hawaii, which, on top of being an exciting place to explore also comes with a pretty hefty dose of jet lag for this East Coaster, I flew to Hawaii a day earlier than I normally would have. After traveling for more than 12 hours I was exhausted, but I was also starving, so I headed to the outdoor restaurant, called Burger in Paradise, right next to the hotel. It was about two o'clock local time, so it wasn't busy. In fact, there was only one gentleman there, sitting at the bar watching the Red Sox game on television. Because I am a huge baseball fan—in fact, at the time I was still living right across the street from Fenway Park—I sat down and started talking to him.

I learned that although he was from New Jersey, he was an avid Red Sox fan. I mentioned that when they did the aerial shots from the blimp you could see my condo. We found out we were both there for the same conference. Over the course of the hour or so that we chatted, he mentioned that he would be staying on after the conference to visit Maui where his girlfriend was joining him, and that he was going to propose. When my bill came he refused to let me pay, as there was no way he was going to meet another Red Sox fan halfway around the world and not treat her. I thanked him, told him I'd look for him at the conference over the next few days, and headed back to my hotel room to crash.

The next morning I got up early to tour Pearl Harbor. As I stood on the shore and looked out at the USS Arizona memorial, I heard someone call my name. I turned around and there was my friend from the day before. We spent the morning together taking in that somber memorial and then joked how two chance encounters in two days must mean that we were supposed to be friends.

I spent the next three days at the conference and didn't see him one more time while I was there. A few weeks after the conference I reached out to him to ask how the proposal went. He told me how his fiancé had been surprised, and how she had said yes. He mentioned that his work took him to Boston a couple times a year, so the next time he was in town we would get together for wine (by this time we knew that we were both wine snobs and had compared wine clubs). Now we get together once or twice a year whenever he is in Boston or I am in New York. We've introduced each other to friends in our networks and made strategic introductions for each other over the years.

This is a beautiful story that shows the power of making it a point to meet people when you go to conferences. It doesn't have to get deeper to prove my point. But it does. Somehow this friend and I always seem to think of each other at pivotal times, like the time I was sitting in a johnnie in the waiting room of a healthcare facility, holding my phone while I waited to have a cranial MRI.

About a week before I had lost the hearing in my right ear. The doctors said this meant I either had a viral infection in my ear, or I had a tumor in my brain that had grown large enough to affect my hearing. On this day, the doctors would inject a dye into my bloodstream and then give me an MRI to determine if I had a brain tumor. I don't know why I had my phone in my hand. To be honest I probably wasn't even allowed to have it with me. I was just sitting there, clutching my phone and trying not to think about what might happen, when I got a text message from my friend.

"Hey, how are you?"

I thought about replying that I was great, busy as usual, blah blah blah, but something told me to tell him the truth.

"I'm sitting in the hospital waiting to have an MRI to see if I have a brain tumor."

Immediately my phone rang. He asked if I was serious. I told him yes, and about the hearing loss. Then he told me that this happened to his sister-in-law, and that she was diagnosed with a brain tumor, and that if I needed anything that he would be there for me, that he had information and resources should I need them. It made me feel so much better in that very tense moment. I am still in awe that I developed such a deep connection to a person whom I simply sat next to and started talking to at a bar in Hawaii.

(I didn't end up having a brain tumor. I had a viral infection in my ear, and a previously undiagnosed inner ear disease, which still plagues me to this day but is totally manageable.)

If I were to tell you all the stories of all of the relationships I created by attending conferences, this chapter would never end. But it has to, so suffice to say, conferences are, like, wicked important.

CONFERENCES ARE TAX-DEDUCTIBLE WORK DISGUISED AS FUN!

One conference I go to each year generally starts on the first Sunday in October. Instead of the consultants trying to put together competing dinners we all decided to band together and have a football party every year. We don our team football jerseys and head out to a local sports bar and watch the game together. It's now a tradition over ten years strong. Getting to drink beer, eat nachos, watch football, and call it work? I'm in!

Remember in Chapter 2 when I said that I love wine and belong to a number of wine clubs? At a recent conference I attended in Seattle I was able to hire a driver to take me and nine of my clients and networking friends to Woodinville for an afternoon of wine tasting and visiting the wineries I belong to. It was so much fun, ten of us spending the afternoon together drinking wine and then having lunch together. At lunch we asked fun non-work-related questions and everyone had to answer. Things like, what one crime are you dying (no pun intended) to know who did it? What could you write a book about? What secret talent do you have that no one knows? Wine, food, thought-provoking conversation—what's not to love?

I have so many more fun conference stories, but I want you to go out and make your own stories. There is no shortage of conferences for you to attend. You could literally go to a conference every week. Don't do that. Spend some time thinking about what you want to get out of attending a conference. Is it to meet potential clients? If yes, then research the conferences that are available in your industry that your potential clients attend. For example, when I was the academic business development director for an international architecture firm, I attended conferences across the United States that were specifically for campus planners, university business officers, college and university physical plant administrators, and heads of schools.

Now that I am an entrepreneur and the CEO of my own company, I look to attend conferences where I can learn from other entrepreneurs and business owners, helping me navigate the hurdles of owning my own business.

There is no hard and fast rule about how many conferences you should attend every year. The key is to look for conferences that you can attend year after year so that you start to build the same connections to clients and contemporaries that I have described above.

My only caveat about conferences is that, as powerful as they are, they are only a piece of your overall networking and business development strategy. You should never put all your eggs in one basket, but conferences are a pretty solid basket to put some of them in.

You should also not invest in a conference a single time and expect the floodgate of opportunities to bust wide open from that sole attendance. You may need to start establishing a presence at your industry conferences to begin to see the rewards of your investment. Conferences are a long-term strategy, but are always worth the time and effort.

CHAPTER 4 TO-DOS:
MAKE A PLAN FOR YOUR NEXT CONFERENCE

1. Research which conferences are available to you in your target market.
2. Determine what you would like to achieve by attending the conference; is it to expand your industry connections, meet potential clients, or perhaps as a growth and learning opportunity for yourself.
3. Reach out to your network to see who might be attending.
4. Register, book your hotel, and see if you can share your travel with another attendee.
5. Create a daily schedule for yourself including all of the keynotes, presentations, and networking/social events you will be attending.
6. Buy more business cards.
7. Schedule follow-up time in your calendar and make it a priority to connect with the people you met within 24-48 hours of the conference ending.

8. Record your thoughts about the conference with tips for the next year so that you can build on the momentum you create year after year.

CONNECTING VIRTUALLY

In October of 2019, I free fell 111 meters off of the Victoria Falls bridge in Zambia. Crazy, right? Believe me, I know. That is a feat that would scare the shit out of anyone—and for me, the fear that I might be the first person to ever shit themselves while jumping off that bridge was *real*. I know that I could possibly literally have been the first to evacuate my bowels on the way down because I asked every single person working on that platform if anyone had ever done it. They all assured me that no, it had never happened. ("Yet," I kept thinking to myself.)

This story gets even more cray-cray (and it doesn't involve poop, you'll be relieved to know): I tandem jumped off that bridge with a woman that I met through a mutual network connection only a couple years before.

It all started when this woman was seated next to a friend of mine, John, at an industry dinner—they sort of knew each other in that they had traded emails back and forth, but they had never met in person. So it was serendipity that they were at the same table. At the dinner they made a date to have coffee in order to learn more about each other's businesses and see how they could help each other. John is a tremendous connector who cares deeply about the people in his network. He always asks how he can be of service to his connections before he leaves a meeting with them. On this particular day when he asked Shannon that question she said, "Can you introduce me to a kick-ass female? It doesn't matter what industry, just someone from your network."

The next day I received an email in my inbox from John that is a great example of an introduction email that stops the recipients in their tracks and makes them want to meet each other, pronto. It read:

Subject: Boom!

Julie, when my close colleague Shannon asked about an introduction to a kick@ss female, only one name popped right to my mind. Shannon, Julie is just what you asked for, maybe more. She understands relationships, adding value, and truly has no competition anywhere in the rearview mirror.

With this email I'd like to suggest that the two of you meet for coffee. I'd be honored to join the two of you, but would like you to set the date with me attending NOT as a prerequisite.

You're both athletic, energetic, and really cool people.
Can't wait to hear where it leads.

As with any intro I make, the industry is irrelevant. I'm matching solely on energy level here.
Gratefully yours,
John

With an introduction like that, how could we not clear our schedules and find a time to meet, immediately?

We met for coffee a couple of days later. As we compared our lists, the similarities just kept coming: runner, skier, world traveler, wine snob, check, check, check. On top of that, we discovered that we lived only two miles from each other.

Our one-hour meeting quickly turned into three. We wanted to keep talking, but we both had lunch appointments to get to, so we picked a date right then and there to get our husbands together and all have dinner together. The rest is history. (She clearly became such a good friend that she was not even worried about the possibility of me shitting myself while strapped to her body—well, maybe just a little bit, but she didn't let that stop her!)

In the two years that we have known each other, we have: traveled to California to visit and compare our wine clubs, dressed as matching unicorns for Reggae Fest at Sugarloaf ski mountain in Maine, gone great white shark cage diving in Gansbaai and seen the big five (and then some) on safari in Sabi Sands, both in South Africa, and jumped off the Victoria Falls bridge together. If Shannon and I are almost the same person, the same goes for our husbands, who have become good friends over the past two years as well.

It all stemmed from that one simple email. Talk about *boom!*

It's important to note that John did not make this introduction with the thought of reciprocation in mind. He simply wanted to connect two people he thought should know each other. That's how, with the purest of intentions, he made our friendship possible, and why I will forever be grateful to him. Of course, the fact that he brought such an important person into my life naturally makes me want to look for opportunities to repay him—either with a job referral, or a hot tip on something happening in the industry that might be good for him to know, or just checking in with him to offer my support whenever he crosses my mind. It's not that taking care of your network is a tit-for-tat game; it's just that when you do something to help others, they naturally want to help you in return. It's not quid pro quo, it's win-win.

As much as I love to meet people at events, sometimes you need a more strategic way to connect with others that doesn't require you to be in the same room at the same time. In this chapter, we'll cover how to use strategic introductions, personalized emails, and LinkedIn to help you build your network.

THE POWER OF THE STRATEGIC INTRODUCTION

Making strategic introductions is something that people often don't give much thought to, but it's a vital piece of building a supportive network. As John said in his email, you don't even have to introduce two people because they work in the same industry or because one of them is looking for a job—the best introductions are simply energetic matches. How can you help people surround themselves with people who care about them and are invested in each other's success?

Think about the strategic introductions you can make for the people in your network. For everyone in your Top 5, and Circle of 15 certainly, and even in your 50, think to yourself, *Do I know anyone who could benefit from being introduced to this person? Or, the flip side, do I know anyone it would be beneficial for this person to meet?* That's all it takes to start weaving the strands of your network web tighter together while helping others grow their network at the same time.

When your relationships are strong enough and you have invested enough time in them, you are 100 percent allowed to ask for a strategic introduction. Here's how:

- Know who you would like to be introduced to and why. If you don't have a specific person in mind, as Shannon didn't, you can know what type of person you'd like to be connected to—in Shannon's case, that was a kickass female.

- Know who within your network has the strongest connection to that person. An introduction from a Top 5 person will go a lot further than an introduction from someone the other person doesn't know particularly well or hasn't talked to in a long time.

- When you make the ask, don't just say, "Hey can you connect me to so and so?" without letting them know why you would appreciate the connection, and what you might possibly be able to offer to the person they are connecting you to.

- Include information that your connection can easily send to their contact; this information will provide context for the introduction and make it easy for them to send along or copy and paste without too much hassle.

- Be respectful if your contact doesn't feel comfortable making the introduction. There are a number of reasons why that might be the case. Don't take it personally, simply look at your network and determine who else might be able to assist you.

To inspire you, here's an example of an email that requests an introduction:

Hello [Insert Name Here],
Great seeing you at the awards gala last week; it's always such a fun event. Congrats on the award–it's certainly well deserved. I know you are [friends with, connected to, used to work with] [insert name here], and I would greatly appreciate an introduction via email if you are comfortable doing so. Her company recently received a grant for employee training and I know that she is looking for local female speakers. I'd love to discuss with

her some amazing workshops that I have been able to facilitate over the years that might be beneficial to her and her employees.

If you are open to it, I have included a blurb below with information on the workshops that you could easily send along with the email.
Cheers,
Julie B

Blurb for you to send:

Hello [insert name here],
I am emailing you to connect you to a good friend of mine, Julie Brown. Julie provides business development and networking workshops to companies in our industry. She has aided in the growth of numerous local companies by giving their employees the tools to build lasting relationships that result in increased business.

Even if you don't have the opportunity to work together, I think you would both benefit from getting to know each other, as you have a number of things in common including skiing, tequila, and raucous laughter.

I'll let this email serve as the introduction, you can take it from here.
Best,
[Insert Name Here]

See, not so hard, right? It also makes it incredibly easy for your contact to reach out, which is more than just polite; it makes it a lot more likely that they'll actually send the email as everyone has more than enough on their plates already and sometimes just having to take the time to think for 10 minutes means something doesn't get done.

HOW TO REACH OUT TO SOMEONE YOU DON'T SHARE A CONNECTION WITH

Over the course of your networking and business development journey, there will inevitably be people you will need to reach out to without the benefit of a warm introduction from a shared connection. Luckily, email makes it easy to do so. The problem is that we all already get way more emails than we could ever respond to. The solution? Craft that email so that it introduces you in such a thoughtful and compelling way that the recipient is bound to respond.

It's not as hard as it might seem. Here's how you do it.

START WITH RESEARCH

The single most important thing when you are trying to cold email someone is to do as much research as you can, not only regarding the company they work at, but also the person as a whole.

Use your research to shine a light on the commonalities you share with the other person in your email. Remember, as we covered in Chapter 2, when you discover what you have in common with other people, it increases the surface area that you have to form a connection with someone else.

STATE YOUR ASK

Why are you reaching out to them? Succinctly tell them why you are trying to connect. It's not being pushy—they are going to be wondering what you want from them, so by stating it clearly, you are relieving them of trying to figure it out.

Here's an example for you: I had been trying to find a way to connect with the owner of an architecture firm for a while—one of my clients offered in-office educational units for architecture firms, and he wanted to see if this person was interested in having him come in.

Everyone I reached out to for a warm introduction told me that this particular owner was "very hard to get to." So, since I wasn't going to be able to get a personal intro, I started my research.

I scoured the internet for information on him. He wasn't on Facebook, or Instagram. He barely had a profile on LinkedIn. He wasn't a ghost, but he was close to it.

The only avenue for information that I had on him was via his firm website. I read every word and analyzed every picture. And then, there it was, a small picture of him skiing down a slope. He was wearing Volkl skis. This, *this* was my commonality to him. Not only was I a skier, I too rode Volkls. It was all I had, so I used it. Below is the email that I sent.

B,

Greetings! I noticed in your bio picture on your website that you ride Volkls. I had always ridden Volkls until this year when I switched over to Solomons...I ski in VT every weekend—where do you call ski home?

I consult with [CLIENT]. Together, we offer a number of AIA Accredited CEU Lunch and Learns and I was wondering if you and your team would be interested in any of the following presentations. If interested perhaps I could work with your assistant to get something scheduled at your office?

AIA CEU Lunch and Learns
[Workshop 1]
[Workshop 2]
[Workshop 3]

I look forward to hearing from you.
Cheers,
JB

This was the email that I got back.

Hi JB (I assume that is OK as it is your 'signature' below),
No one has ever sent me an email, especially as an introduction email, with reference to the skis in my bio image. That took some research and effort. Good for you! And how can I not reply to a fellow skier? But Solomons? Really? Just kidding! Congrats for getting up to ski each weekend in NE [New England]. I did that for many years. One must be a trooper, what with the variety of weather that Mother Nature throws at us.

My NE ski home had been in North Conway for many years. In recent years, I have been fortunate to be hosted at Steamboat by ski friends. This year I was there for almost four weeks. It makes my professional life a bit hectic, but it is worth it. And I'm seeking to ski a bit more each year. Day trips in NE are to Sunapee or North Conway.

We would be interested in your Lunch and Learn. I suggest that you reconnect with me the week of June 25. Our office manager, M, is away on vacation right now. That makes my schedule a bit more frantic. So let's wait until she gets back and schedule a day and time for your visit to Topsfield.

Nicely done on the sleuthing.
Cheers,
B

His response shows how little effort most people usually put into reaching out to another person. No one had ever sent an email introduction like mine, and I'm guessing he'd never written a response like the one he sent me. It was filled with personal information, all offered in response to one well-researched dopamine-inducing question: "Where do you call ski home?"

Even better, he agreed to meet with my client, and even congratulated me for my "sleuthing." This was a person who I had been told over and over that I would not be able to connect with because he never responded to emails. Well, he responded to mine, because I took the time to learn more about him and discover what we had in common before reaching out.

How many emails would you go back and do differently? How many more email responses would you have if you had taken the time to find your common thread with the other person? It's not too late. Go back and look at the emails that you have sent that have gone unanswered and discover how you can research your contact and write a more compelling email, one that deserves to be answered.

USING LINKEDIN TO BUILD YOUR NETWORK IN A MEANINGFUL WAY (YES, IT'S POSSIBLE)

Currently, LinkedIn is the single biggest online business-networking site available to you; it has half a billion users in more than 200 countries, and for the most part it's totally free. You should 100 percent be using LinkedIn in your networking and business development strategy. If you're not, you are missing out.

That being said, you can't just go on there and start trying to connect with people willy-nilly. It's not a popularity contest, people, and there's little to no value of "linking in" with people whom you don't know anything about in real life and who don't know anything about you.

Also, if you aren't thoughtful about the information you present on LinkedIn, you could just be shooting yourself in the foot because you'll essentially be broadcasting to the world, "Hey, I don't really give a shit about LinkedIn, I'm just here because it exists and somebody told me I should." That's not the impression you want to give, is it? I didn't think so.

So before we talk about how to use LinkedIn to make meaningful connections, there are a couple of housekeeping things you need to tend to before you start connecting with people on the platform. (I've put all the tips I'm about to share with you into a checklist that's part of the free workbook that's available at juliebrownbd.com/reallygoodshit—be sure to download so you can print this out and have it handy as you're working on your profile.)

Treat LinkedIn like it's your virtual business card and your resume. This means having an appropriate and up-to-date professional headshot. A selfie won't do; a picture of you at your best friend's wedding won't do; a picture of you ten years and ten pounds ago won't do. Have a professional head-shot taken, one of you as you look right now, and make it your profile. Then, next year, update that puppy so that you stay current. (Also, updating your profile picture is a great opportunity for you to show up in people's feeds and to have them reach out to you, or at least bring you to the top of their mind on a regular, if extended, basis.)

Make sure your professional title, current company, and location are all correct. I see so many people who continue to use LinkedIn but forget to update their basic information. Don't do that.

And now, let's go over the parts of your profile that require a little more thought:

ABOUT

For your About section, make sure that you not only include what you do for a living and the problems that you solve for your clients, but also what you like to do when you are not at work. Remember, we are 360-degree people, and we are trying to connect with people in as many ways as possible.

EXPERIENCE

For each of your previous positions, include the dates of employment and a short description of your role and responsibilities.

EDUCATION

Include your learning, both formal and informal; with years of attendance.

SKILLS AND ENDORSEMENTS

Create a list of skills that you have, so that people in your network can endorse you for them.

RECOMMENDATIONS

You can never have enough recommendations. Ask the people in your network to recommend you for the work that you do. My LinkedIn profile page is full of recommendations from the people in my network, whether from people that I have mentored or been mentored by, my contemporaries, past colleagues, or past clients. Every recommendation adds to the credibility of my work and will do the same for you.

INTERESTS, CAUSES, AND GROUPS

Further fill out your bio by listing your business and personal interests, the causes that you are passionate about, and the LinkedIn groups that you are involved in.

Now that your bio is on point, you can begin to reach out and make connections within the platform.

HOW TO CONNECT ON LINKEDIN

Connecting on LinkedIn has all the same rules as connecting via email, you just have a smaller character count with which to make your case. Here are some guidelines on how to do it:

RESEARCH THEIR BIO

Just like if you were going to connect via email, learn as much as you can about this person. That of course means reading their profile, but it also means seeing what you can find online via company bios, articles, etc. Once when I was trying to reach out to a developer on LinkedIn, I discovered in his company bio that he was a big fan of hard cider. I made sure to include that fact in my request, and I promised to bring him cider from Vermont when we met face to face (which I totally did).

DISCOVER YOUR SHARED CONNECTIONS

Just like asking for a personal introduction, discover who you have in common and then ask that person if you can use their name when you send your invite. Always ask; don't just assume you can use someone's name—that's a total douche move.

WRITE A COMPELLING REASON TO CONNECT

Never, never, NEVER send a generic "I'd like to connect with you on LinkedIn" request. I have dozens if not hundreds of outstanding invitations to connect on LinkedIn that I will simply not accept. And it's not because I'm some self-important asshole. I don't accept invitations from anyone that I have not met in person, or if I don't know why they want to connect with me. I do this because I value my relationships, I put time and effort into nurturing them, and I will protect the strength of my network from people who don't understand the value of real connections.

Below is an example of a LinkedIn request that came to me from a person I had not yet met, but whom I was happy to connect with because their personalization let me know why they wanted to connect.

> Hi Julie,
>
> I had coffee with JF the other day. She mentioned that I should reach out to connect with you. I am new to the industry and she mentioned you would be a great person to meet with. Please let me know if I can take you out to coffee when your schedule allows.
>
> Thank you,
>
> C

This request does a lot of things correctly: They mention a mutual contact who is a friend of mine; they let me know why they wanted to connect (because they are new to the industry); and they initiated an action item—to have coffee together.

Now, here is an example of a LinkedIn request that I sent to a person that one of my clients wanted to meet.

> AM,
>
> I would love to connect. For business, but also because you are one of the hockey dads for my best friend's son (CL). HL says you are the best! I consult with a number of firms here in the city; there may be synergy between a couple of them and your firm. Would love to find a time to get together and discuss.
>
> Cheers,
>
> JB

In this request I made sure to say how we are connected through a mutual friend; I stated who I was and why I wanted to meet; and I initiated a next action item. It worked like a charm: He accepted and we set up a time and met the next week.

ONCE THEY ACCEPT YOUR INVITE

It doesn't make any sense to connect with someone on Linke-dIn and then have the story end there. As soon as someone accepts my LinkedIn request, I go to their contact information, copy their email, and then send them a personal email from my email address to theirs so that I can connect with them off of the LinkedIn platform. Some people check LinkedIn sporadically, and I don't want my communication with them to get lost or lose momentum, so I like to get right into their work email inbox. The first thing I do in that email is to thank them for accepting my request and agreeing to connect. I then follow up with additional information about why I wanted to connect, making sure to pepper in the common threads that I have discovered. I end my email with a call to action, by requesting a time to connect by phone or in a face-to-face meeting. I offer dates and times so that the person can easily see when our meeting can fit in their schedule.

The steps outlined above are the best ways to move a connection from a purely virtual platform into an in-person connection. And once you have an in-person connection, really, the sky is the limit for how strong a relationship you can develop, because, as we'll dive into the very next chapter, there is no difference between a work friend and a real friend. This is where networking gets really fun, because it's about building relationships that enrich all parts of your life—even if you don't end up strapping yourself to one of your new friends and plunging 111 meters into the air with them.

CHAPTER 5 TO-DOS:
MAKE YOUR STRATEGIC CONNECTIONS!

1. Ask two people from your network to introduce you to two amazing people from their network.

2. Connect two people from your network together who don't know each other but would totally be a great connection.

3. Go back to any unanswered cold emails, do your research, find your common connections or commonality, and resend them using what you discover.

4. Beef up your LinkedIn bio and then send a compelling LinkedIn request to someone you would like to get to know.

5. Repeat.

WORK FRIENDS ARE REAL FRIENDS

Over the years I have been contacted by a number of women's organizations inquiring if I would come and give a presentation on work-life balance. My answer is always no. Not because I don't like speaking to women's groups. In fact, I love it. It's because work-life balance is a crock of shit.

Yes, you read that right: Work-life balance is a huge crock of shit.

If I were to ask you right now if you are busy, would you respond, *No not me, not busy at all—I'm actually looking for some more shit to do?*

I didn't think so.

We are all so fucking busy.

So, what does that have to do with networking? Surprisingly, more than you think. The hallmark of your success is not that you are "so busy" jamming all of the pieces of your life onto the sides of a big scale and hopefully the sides balance out. Your success will never be defined by how busy you are.

It's not a sin to make money. It's especially not a sin for you to make money because you are wildly successful doing something you love, because you have surrounded yourself with a network of people who are invested in you and help assure your success. And it's not a sin to have all of that and not be killing yourself to achieve it.

The term *work-life balance* suggests that work and life are two completely separate parts of your existence. I'm telling you, in today's over-connected, "internet of things world" they are one and the same. You cannot completely shut off your work brain while you are doing "life" things, nor can you completely disconnect from what's going on in your life while you're at work. There will always be life events that affect your work schedule and work deadlines that affect your free time. Trying to keep them separate, much less balanced, is impossible. Thinking you can will only make you crazy.

Too many people spend their days as two completely different people: the person they are at work, and then the person they are at home or with friends. Maintaining those two selves is a ton of work. It's confusing, and it's exhausting.

Here's a truth for you: When you erase the line that bifurcates your work self and your real self, you can integrate them together into one kick-ass whole self.

For example, I cringe when I hear people use the term "work friends." Are they your friends or aren't they? Why do you have to categorize the friends you make at work differently than you would any of your other friends? Are work friends not real friends? Allow me to answer that: Work friends are 100 percent your real friends. The only reason they don't feel real is that you still have a wall up between your work self and your real self. The friends you make at work don't only belong in your "work" life; they are absolutely allowed in your "real" life. Because they are both part of you.

On the flip side, you are completely allowed to network with your non-work friends. How many "real friends" do you have right now that you have no clue what they do for a living? I bet it's more than you think. Why aren't you getting to know what they do, so that you can be a potential referral source for them? If you have a close friend, and you have no idea what their husband or wife does for a living, you need to ask them so that you can potentially be a part of their network, help them, and be a referral source for them.

All that being said, I understand that it's not as easy as ripping down the curtain between the two halves of your life and voila, you feel balanced. And that we all have stress that stems from work and life. The thing about life is that none of us are getting out of it alive. Your resume and your obituary shouldn't be the same document. Most of us have to work, and most of us would like to find some way to fit life into our world as well. Not just fit it in, but be really present while we are there.

Here are some thoughts on how each of us can begin to make that happen.

- **Try to do something you actually like.** You spend dozens of hours a week at your job. Loving what you do is a good way to not resent the time you have to spend working. That in and of itself will make your life feel more "balanced."

    I work all day, most nights, and some weekends, yet I always feel in balance because I truly love what I do and I work with people I have genuine connections with and with whom I love spending time.

    I realize this can take a while to make happen if you're in a job or an industry that you truly don't like. The good news is that all the things you're learning in this book will help you develop and strengthen the network that will help you find that job you actually enjoy.

- **Think outside the box with networking.** There are so many ways to network; it doesn't just have to be at events. Find ways to actively combine your life with your work and your work with your life. I love when networking feels like play but I still get a shit-ton of networking in. Some examples of this include:
  - **Golf** is a fantastic way to be outside, get some fresh air, get a little exercise in, and still network your face off. I love golf for networking. And ladies please do not be intimidated by golf; men suck at it too, you're gonna be just fine out there. Because golf is such an important business tool, and wanting the women in our industry to feel comfortable learning how to play, a couple of years ago a handful of ladies from my industry created our own golf league. During the summer we golf together every Tuesday, and catch up at the 19th hole afterwards. A lot of great networking comes out of this type of camaraderie.
  - **Skiing** is one of my all-time favorite ways to network. All of the industry groups that I belong to put together a ski day—a bus picks you up in the morning, you get to network all day in a super fun environment, and by the time the day is over you've made a bunch of new friends and gotten a full workout in. Win, win, win.
  - **Yoga and wine is just an excellent combo.** So many of the women in my industry love yoga and wine, so I like to get a few girls together for a yoga class followed by a glass of wine or what I like to call Detox/Retox.

- **Stop trying to "have it all."** The idea that you can have it all—and, more specifically, that you are supposed to be able to do it all—can really stress a bitch out. The idea that if we aren't accomplishing all the things, all the time, all at once means that we are somehow failing at life can make anyone feel that they don't measure up. But this idea is bullshit. So stop being so damn hard on yourself for not being able to fit everything in everyday. Allow yourself to be okay with the fact that sometimes everything won't get done. Some days you won't get your workout in, some days you won't be able to make that networking event, some days you'll feed your kids crap fast food for dinner because you just don't have the time to make a healthy meal. The world will not end. You are not a failure. You do not suck.

  Also, this takes work but stop comparing yourself or measuring your self-worth against someone else who seems to be able to do it all. You have no idea what doing it all costs that person. When I notice that my stress levels are rising and I feel out of balance, I check in to see if I'm trying to do everything. I usually am. Then I give myself permission to let some stuff slide, focus on what I truly enjoy, and I'm back to feeling good.

- **Make sure your schedule has room for what you need to be your best.** Each Sunday look at your schedule for the coming week. Write down what you need to accomplish at work, what networking opportunities you will make time for, and your non-negotiable personal, family, or friend time that has to happen. Schedule each of these in your calendar. Block the time out so that you can be sure that you don't accidentally schedule something that conflicts with these must-dos.

For example, I block out the hour from 5:30-6:30 each morning to run, work out, or ride the Peloton. This is non-negotiable for me, because my workout is my moving meditation. Then, when someone asks me if I can meet at 7 or even 7:30 in the morning I don't even have to think about it; I decline and say that my first available meeting time is 8 am. This way I do not resent a meeting or event because it took away from the personal time that I need to start my day off on the right foot, and it hasn't forced me to try and jam that workout into another part of the day.

We are all entitled to time off the clock; by scheduling my workouts for 5:30 am, I'm making damn sure that work doesn't creep into my me time. Think about what you need to feel your best—is it working out, downtime, dinner with friends, being home with your kids by a certain time?

It's also important to think about when you won't do something. For me, even though I love networking and commit to attending networking events twice a week, I have learned that everything in my life goes better when I don't network on Monday nights.

Attending an event on Monday night can make me tired and less productive for the rest of the week. This leaves Monday nights open for yoga class, taking my nephew to his ski lessons, dinner with friends, or my activity of choice—Netflix binging. That means I can pick from Tuesday, Wednesday, and Thursday to be my "event nights," and I still have one other work weeknight open for whatever I would like to do.

- **Don't resent the achievements of others.** We are human, and sometimes we can have a negative reaction to someone else's success. I know that I am guilty of this—of getting in a funk because I think others are getting somewhere faster than me. This attitude is never going to serve you in a positive way. We need to celebrate the achievements, big and small, of everyone in our network. Your network is a living, breathing organism; individual successes are indeed shared success. No one does this alone, so take joy in the achievements of others. Your time is coming.

SET YOURSELF UP FOR SUCCESS—EVERY DAY

A big source of stress is thinking that you can accomplish more than is humanly possible in a day. If you give yourself a list of 20 to-dos you'll never be able to finish; it's an invitation to beat yourself up.

Studies suggest that five is actually the magic number of things you can realistically expect to accomplish in a work day. So each night, ideally before you stop working for the day so that your brain is still in work mode, make a list of the five things you need to get done by the end of the next day. Really stick to only five things—any more than that and you'll get overwhelmed, which only hinders your productivity.

Having this list helps you get right to work in the morning and eliminates the hours you might otherwise spend on determining what to do next. This practice has been a real time-saver for me, helping me stay focused and on top of my deliverables to clients.

MULTI-TASKING IS MAKING YOU A DUMBASS

Another great way to lose a lot of time and suck at your job is to multitask. So many people think that they are good at multitasking—some people even list "ability to multitask" on their resume as a strength.

That's a load of horse shit. It has been scientifically proven that doing multiple things at once isn't just distracting—it actually lowers your IQ three times more than smoking marijuana. In short, it makes you dumber.

Now, I'm not against smoking weed—and here in the great state of Massachusetts it's 100 percent legal to do so—but imagine being really, really, really stoned and then trying to focus on something important. That's what is happening to your brain every time you try to multitask.

We as humans are quickly losing the ability to focus. The average time an American worker spends on a task before being interrupted is one minute and 15 seconds. The average person checks their phone 80 times per day. This is crazy.

Just because you can do more than one thing at the same time doesn't mean that you should.

The negative effects of trying to multitask include:

- a 50 percent increase in how long it takes to accomplish a single task
- 50 percent more errors
- a 40 percent drop in productivity across the board

So how can you stop multitasking in our overtaxed and overtasked world, when your phone and inbox are dinging every few seconds?

Here are five ways to help avoid distractions:

1. Put your phone where you can't see it. If you are at your desk, put it in a drawer so that you are not constantly

tempted to touch it. No touchy! If that doesn't work, set your phone to "do not disturb."

2. Avoid desktop distractions. When you are working on a project on your computer, turn off your notifications—this means no email or text pop ups.

3. Schedule your distraction time; meaning, have set times throughout the day to check your email, text, and voicemail. For example, you might check them when you first get into the office, right before your lunch break, and just before you leave the office.

4. Don't be afraid to say no. You are likely already trying to fit too much into too little time, so say no to a task that you cannot fully take on. Doing a task half-assed isn't going to help anyone.

5. Now, this one is difficult, especially for me, but here it is: Be mindful. I have a meditation app on my phone and on days when it is particularly hard for me to concentrate, I take 10-15 minutes to go through a guided meditation. It's hard to walk away from a busy schedule even for 15 minutes, but these short meditations help me refocus and be more productive. I realize the irony of telling you to hide your phone and then telling you to use your phone to play a meditation app—but this is one instance when your phone can indeed help you focus. So there.

2020 FORCED US TO MERGE WORK AND LIFE—LET'S KEEP IT THAT WAY

I had largely finished this book and was in final editing mode when the first Covid-19 (the respiratory disease caused by the coronavirus) cases started to appear in the United States. Soon after that, restaurants closed, schools closed, all sporting events were cancelled, and then all non-essential businesses were closed. This forced the folks who worked for non-essential businesses, and who still had a job, to work from home.

The home now became the epicenter of our entire lives. It became the classroom, office, gym, restaurant, bar. It took on the life of all the things we were no longer allowed to do outside of its walls. It forced us to let everyone—friends, coworkers, strangers—into our homes in a virtual setting. We did this through Zoom meetings, Facebook Live events, webinars, Instagram stories, and Google Hangouts. This virus stripped us all down to something so very basic and yet so true: We saw that we are all multidimensional humans. Yes, we have jobs, but in our virtual meetings during this time we were given the opportunity to meet the husbands, wives, extended families, cats, and dogs that make up "life" for our coworkers and network. The pandemic forced us to blend our "work" and our "life" together, in the same place, and have that place be completely visible to all to see. I for one believe that's how it should be. I hope we always remember this glimpse into the lives we were allowed to see, to remember that we are all human beings with big, messy, full lives outside of work.

Now, I want you to repeat after me: *Work-life balance doesn't exist.* Instead, aim for work-life *integration* by planning for and sticking to your non-negotiables, not wasting countless hours procrastinating or multitasking, and remembering that it is okay to show parts of your "life" at work. You can do this. And when you do, it will be even easier to be generous, kind, and receptive to the people around you—something that, wouldn't you know it?, we'll cover in the next chapter.

CHAPTER 6 TO-DOS:
BLEND YOUR WORK AND LIFE

1. Have a conversation with your friends about their careers; learn more about what they do.

2. Hang out with a "work friend" outside of work.

3. Discover or plan a fun networking activity.

4. Set your work, networking, and non-negotiable time in your schedule each week.

5. Create a list of five things to accomplish at work each day (and stick to it).

CHAPTER 7

BEING AN ASSHOLE WON'T GET YOU VERY FAR

"It is truly a privilege to live by what I call the 'no asshole' rule. I don't do business with assholes. I don't care how much money they are offering me, or what project. Life is too short. Quality of life is important. I'm fortunate to collaborate with a lot of people who I respect and like, and I'd like to keep it that way."
—Anthony Bourdain, *GQ* interview, January 18, 2019

Anthony Bourdain committed suicide less than six months after this interview was published. I remember hearing the news and thinking to myself, *Why did he do that? He had the most amazing life!*

And then in the next breath realizing, everyone really is fighting some secret battle you know nothing about.

This is why kindness and empathy can be your superpower—they help you connect with people in a crazy world. And they help you stand out, because putting these skills at the forefront of how you approach others absolutely flies in the face of how most asshat people go about doing business. Their mentality, whether it's when they walk into a networking event or client meeting, or are meeting someone for the first time, is always, "What's in it for me?" People like this are so consumed with trying to figure out what they can get out of a relationship that they forget that they have to earn it, and they are earning it from people who have real lives, which means they also have real problems.

Empathy and kindness help you earn trust, and earn it with far less stress and effort than trying to score a sale. Being an entitled asshole, thinking that everyone owes you something and that you don't have to give first will derail you every time.

In his book *Emotional Intelligence*, Daniel Goleman states that, "Those who have just enough IQ to get into a decent university, but have stellar EQ, are the ones that rake in the most cash."

This Dan Goleman fellow is the cat's ass when it comes to understanding emotional intelligence and its effect on success. His research from years of studies within hundreds of companies shows that for jobs of all kinds, emotional intelligence is twice as important an ingredient of outstanding performance as cognitive ability and technical skill combined.

What the research shows is that IQ and your technical skill set (architect, lawyer, doctor) are considered "threshold skills" and only account for about eight or nine percent of success each. But the emotional skill set, or EQ, has twice, as in two times, the factor of success as IQ and technical skills *combined*.

Did you hear that? Twice as much as cognitive ability and technical skills...*combined*.

Before we get any further into this, let's go over some basic definitions.

ASSHOLE

1. Literally, a person's anus.
2. Metaphorically, a stupid, irritating, or contemptible person.

INTELLIGENCE QUOTIENT (IQ)

A measure of your ability to reason and solve problems. Your IQ is fixed at birth. No amount of studying will increase it. If this fact distresses you, fear not, because a high IQ number is not a predictor of success.

PERSONALITY

Personality is the combination of characteristics or qualities that form an individual's distinctive character. Personality is another attribute that is fixed at birth. Anyone who has kids knows that distinct personalities begin to reveal themselves in children almost immediately. This also means that an extroverted child will not grow up to become an introverted adult or vice versa. I put this in here because people have a tendency to confuse personality and EQ.

EMOTIONAL INTELLIGENCE (EQ)

A measure of your self-awareness, empathy, and ability to deal sensitively with other people. Emotional intelligence is the combination of emotions created within the limbic brain and how our rational brain uses those emotions.

Goleman's research goes on to show that within different fields like law, medicine, and business management, each professional has had to pass the same intellectual barriers to entry. Meaning your smarts and your ability to do your job aren't enough to make you stand out, or be more successful than all the other people who have the same "threshold skills" as you.

Goleman also states, "Rainmakers at law firms bring in new clients not because of their LSAT scores, but because of the kind of people they are—charismatic, likable, trustworthy. Intellect and technical expertise get you so far, but it's the human qualities that make you a star."

So, since EQ is what it takes to make you a star let's learn a little more about it, shall we?

There are five elements of emotional intelligence:

Self-Awareness: You know how you are feeling all of the time, and how your feelings affect other people.

Self-Regulation: You have the ability to control your emotions and actions.

Self-Motivation: You are able to put off short-term rewards for long-term success.

Empathy: You have the ability to identify with other people and understand their wants and needs.

Social Skills: You can build and sustain relationships, work positively with other people, and manage conflict effectively.

If you want to break it down even further, there are two main skills for emotional intelligence:

Personal Competence: Awareness of your own emotions and how you manage them.

Social Competence: How you read and respond to other people.

What is wonderful about EQ is that it's not fixed at birth. Meaning every single person has the ability to increase it with time and with experience. And it's a damn good thing you can work on it, because I recently took an online EQ test and scored a mere 66 out of 100. I essentially failed. *Me*, the person who teaches people how to build authentic relationships, with anyone, anywhere, anytime.

I was dumbfounded. How could this be?

Flabbergasted, I set out to learn how I could fix this, as I know all too well that my future success depends on it.

I read every article on EQ, read every study, watched every TED talk—and there are a shit-ton of TED talks on it, believe me. One particular talk was given by Dr. Travis Bradberry where he outlined what he termed the three silver bullets to increase emotional intelligence. They aren't what you think they are.

You are probably thinking the silver bullets have to do with emotions, and what is in our hearts. If you are, you're wrong. Since emotions are generated in the limbic part of our brain, and then transferred to the rational part of our brain where we determine how we respond to them, the silver bullets are all about the brain and managing what happens inside of it.

I know, I was surprised by this too, but here we go.

SILVER BULLET NUMERO UNO: GET YOUR STRESS UNDER CONTROL

A small amount of intermittent stress is actually good for us it keeps us on our toes and stimulates the brain-producing cells that help with memory. Too much stress, however, will inevitably lead to a lack of self-control. The way you respond to situations when you are at elevated stress levels is completely different than the way you respond when your stress levels are minimal. Not to mention that stress leads to a host of other unpleasant things, like heart disease, depression, obesity, and my personal favorite—grinding your teeth and then paying to have your front teeth remade three times. Good times.

So how can you combat stress?

For one answer to this question we can look to the work being done by Robert A. Emmons, professor of psychology at UC Davis and a leading expert on the science of gratitude.

Emmons suggests that every time you feel stressed, take a moment to stop and think of one thing you are grateful for. This small act has shown the ability to lower the level of the stress hormone cortisol in the brain by 23 percent.

Try it. Right now. In the margin of this book, right over there ——————————————————————>, write something you are grateful for at this moment. I'll do the same.

> *I am grateful that my rescue dogs know that they have found their forever home.*
>
> *And that their paws always smell like Fritos!*

It works, right? Don't tell me you don't feel a smidge better than you did before you wrote down whatever it was that you are grateful for.

Now, if you have gotten this far into this book you've probably gotten the hint that I'm not exactly the hold hands and sing "Kumbaya" kind of girl. I can 100 percent maintain my badass status and still be a grateful person. Being grateful or kind or thoughtful does not make you a pushover or a doormat. In her People's Choice Award speech in November 2019, singer, activist, and winemaker (yes, she owns a vineyard) Pink said, "Kindness today is an act of rebellion."

Make it your rebellion too.

We all hear great things about meditation, and I know that when I listen to my guided meditation app I do feel better, but I'm not going to tell you that you have to meditate everyday because, frankly, I have failed at becoming a regular meditator. I bought the Calm app and I tried, but I just haven't been able to make it part of my daily schedule; I tend to reach for it when I am super stressed out. Like I said, I hear there are amazing benefits to it, not the least of which is less stress and more clarity, but I'm clearly no expert on it and should not be telling you or anyone else how to do it. If you try it and it works for you and you've found a way to make it a daily practice, please reach out to me and share your strategy!

SILVER BULLET DOS: CLEAN UP YOUR SLEEP HYGIENE

The good news is that you probably don't need more sleep, which will probably make you happy to hear since it's hard to find extra minutes, let alone hours, to dedicate to slumber.

You probably need *better* sleep. Here's why: Over the course of our waking hours, toxic proteins naturally build up in the neurons of our brain. Sleep is the body's natural way of removing these toxic proteins and refreshing our brains. Because of this you need to remove anything artificial that you have been using to "help" you sleep: Benadryl, a couple glasses of wine, melatonin, Ambien...etc. These artificial sleep aids interfere with your body's ability to go through normal sleep stages. This not only causes you to wake up groggy, it eliminates the body's ability to remove these toxic proteins.

A couple days after I learned about these toxic proteins (in, you guessed it, a TED talk), a study was released that showed that people with continuous healthy sleep habits had a reduced likelihood of being diagnosed with dementia and/or Alzheimer's. Now I'm not a doctor, but part of me thinks it has something to do with the removal of those toxic proteins during sleep.

If you take melatonin to help you sleep, I want you to stop taking it and simply remove blue light from your nighttime routine. Our bodies will naturally produce melatonin at night if we are exposed to bright (aka blue) light during the day and then dimmed light (more in the red spectrum, like firelight or candlelight) at night. Blue light tells your brain that it's time to be awake, and each night when you spend time on your computer, iPad, or iPhone with the blue light shining in your face, you are signaling to your brain that you are supposed to be awake, so it halts the production of melatonin. Because of this I have instituted my own "no blue light in the bedroom rule," which means that we do not have a television in our bedroom, we do not allow computers or iPads in the bedroom, and all iPhones must be set to Night Shift so the screen produces only warm light from sunset to sunrise.

What does better sleep have to do with EQ? There is a part of our brain called the amygdala, and that bad Larry is responsible for our strongest negative emotions, like anger and rage. Studies find that subjects who have been exposed to sleep deprivation show a 60 percent increase in activity in the amygdala. Let me spell that out for you: a 60 percent increase in the part of the brain that makes you angry and rage-y. I know when I'm angry and in a rage I could literally give zero fucks about what other people are going through. When you are tired and frustrated and not thinking straight it is really hard to see and care about other people. Being in this state makes it unbelievably hard to step outside of your internal feelings and notice how your words or actions affect other people.

I know when I am tired I have less patience for people, I am quick to judge, and I respond in a more sarcastic way than the situation calls for. I also know that when I am tired, it's hard for me to focus on what other people are potentially going through because I am so consumed with how much everything sucks for me and how much I would just love to take a nap.

It's hard to argue with science, so below are two different images showing my personal sleep reports from two different nights. The top represents a night where I followed the sleep hygiene tips: I went to bed early, didn't partake in any sleep aids of any kind (even wine), and eliminated all the blue light in my bedroom.

The bottom represents a night where I had a couple glasses of wine, stayed up too late, and also read a few articles on my iPhone while I was in bed.

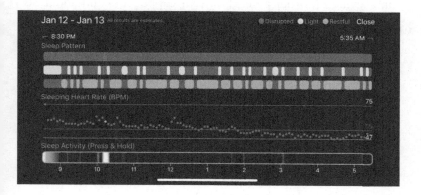

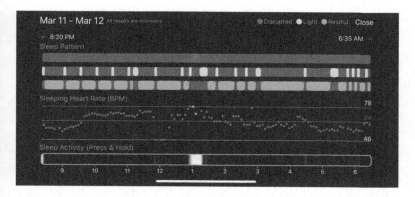

It's more than obvious which activities resulted in a better night's sleep, the kind of sleep that allows you to wake up more rested, with a clear head, and with a greater capacity for emotional intelligence.

SILVER BULLET TRES: REDUCE CAFFEINE INTAKE

The half-life of caffeine is six hours, so ideally you should not have caffeine after 12:00 pm. I know that sucks for a lot of you, but try it and see if it helps with your sleep hygiene and overall feeling of being less jittery around people. I do not have caffeine in my diet due to a congenital heart defect. Every once in a while I'll order a decaf latte or cappuccino and about 30 minutes after drinking it will realize that it was *totally not decaf*. I know this because I'm shaky, on edge, my heart is racing, and I can't sit still!

The fact that every day people fill their bodies with a substance that has the ability to do this to their system is more than just a little scary, especially because most people don't have just one coffee, they have two or three (or more). I've been in the line at Starbucks and heard people order a drink with a quad shot—that's four extra shots of espresso. I guarantee your body does not need that.

Don't get me started on Red Bull; it doesn't give you wings, it gives you the jitters.

Try to limit your caffeine intake after 12:00. If you love a 3:00 pm afternoon coffee, try switching to decaf to determine if you really need the caffeine or you simply enjoy the ritual of an afternoon coffee.

INCREASING EQ THROUGH LIFE EXPERIENCES

We generally become more empathetic as we grow older and have more life experiences with which to relate to other people. Here's an example of how our empathy for others can change over time, simply by experiencing and being a part of something different or new.

Before my sister had her own children I wondered how and why anyone would bring their children to a restaurant. If I was out to dinner, and a family with children happened to be seated next to me, I automatically assumed the children were going to be complete assholes and ruin my meal. I'm sure my face said as much, too. And don't even talk to me about bringing your baby or your kids on an airplane.

I had zero empathy or EQ around what it was like to be a mother, how difficult it must be to go out to dinner, or to make sure your kids are occupied on a long-haul flight. That was until my younger sister became a mother; it was then that I saw how difficult it was to enjoy a meal at a restaurant without everyone expecting one of her kids to have a meltdown.

I then realized how hard it must be for children to deal with the air pressure changes within the cabin of a plane during take off and landing, and how some babies are too young to be able to communicate that their ears hurt, so they cry.

New moms, I got ya. I now have empathy for you, and I promise not to cringe when you sit next to me with your kids at a restaurant or on a plane. I promise to not roll my eyes or say things under my breath, unless your kid is a total asshole and you're not even trying to help them through the situation, then I will still do that.

I mentioned in the introduction that my father was a heroin addict. When I was 33 years old I received a call that he was in hospice, and if I wanted to see him before he passed away I needed to visit him soon. This might be an easy decision for most people, but I hadn't spoken to him in eight years. My father got sober when I was 25. He had missed every part of my life up until that point—every Christmas, every birthday, high school graduation, college graduation, and all the little moments in between. Now that he was sober he wanted to have a relationship with me. I didn't trust him to stay sober and I didn't think he deserved to come back into my life now that I was an adult, so I said no. He subsequently missed me buying my first home, my engagement, and my wedding. He'd never met my husband. So you see, choosing whether or not to visit him in hospice wasn't an easy decision to make. I took 24 hours to collect my thoughts and then decided that I would visit him. I knew he probably had things to say and I wanted to give him the opportunity to say them. He was 57 when he died. The years of alcohol and drug abuse were just too much for his body. He was young. Too young. And as I stood there and saw what his addiction had done to him, and all the things it had taken away from him, I knew in that moment that for all those years, he didn't have a choice. No one in their right mind would choose this. It was in that singular moment that my entire attitude toward addiction changed. I no longer looked at it as a character flaw and a conscious decision to choose drugs over everything else, including friends and family. I now had empathy for everyone fighting this battle, no matter how their addiction started, and what they were addicted to.

I'm not sure what the lesson is here except maybe to learn as much as you can about issues before making a judgment call, or try putting yourself in someone else's shoes before you pass judgment. Yes, that will be hard to do. After all, we are wired to react a certain way. And that's exactly why learning to increase your empathy towards others is paramount to being better at relationships.

INCREASING EQ THROUGH EXERCISE

Since we have the ability to increase our EQ, can we put it on a training regimen, bring it to the gym, make it do some super sets, give it a protein shake, and begin to build up its muscle memory? Yes, we can. So grab your water, grab your towel, and get ready to work it. Here are some exercises that just might pump up your EQ number.

1. **Do something you suck at.** Yeah, we all feel comfortable doing things that we are good at, but what would happen if you took lessons for an activity that you know you suck at? It could be painting, learning a foreign language, playing the piano, whatever. Reminding your brain what it takes to learn something new is a humbling experience, and humility is a huge factor in your ability to empathize.

2. **Go somewhere you don't feel comfortable.** Travel to a place where you don't speak the language. Participate in cultures that are foreign to you, and begin to understand the world outside of your immediate cultural comfort zone. If traveling isn't in your budget, go to a restaurant to try the food from another culture. Even small steps are helpful.

3. **Ask for honest feedback.** Ask your friends and family for honest feedback about your relationship skills. Specifically, you can ask what they really like about your skills and also what they don't. We need to be able to grow, and we won't know what we need to work on if we don't ask honestly.

4. **Don't judge; instead, discover.** Ask honest questions and listen wholeheartedly. The more you know about others, the deeper your connections to them can become. When you ask the questions that allow you to discover the struggles that others are facing, only then can you begin to understand how you can be of service to them.

UNDERSTANDING WHAT YOU NEED TO WORK ON

One way to increase your EQ is to understand what parts of your emotional skill set need work. Taking an EQ test can help you do just that. Visit any of the following sites for a free online EQ test, or simply Google "free online EQ test" and pick one.

https://globalleadershipfoundation.com/geit/eitest.html

https://www.ihhp.com/free-eq-quiz/

https://www.psychologytoday.com/us/tests/personality/emotional-intelligence-test

A CRUCIAL PART OF EQ: VULNERABILITY

By 2010 I had spent 11 years in academic architecture and construction. Over those years, I formed a solid network around me within the industry that I used to share information, uncover leads, and create strategic introductions. This was a trying time, but it was made easier due to the collective power of my network.

What I didn't have at this time was the same kind of network within the high-end residential market, which was my husband Chris' market. I was faced with the fact that I was the one who pushed him to go out on his own. I had told him to just focus on being an architect, I would focus on bringing in the work. I feared that I would fail him. Every day I stressed over how I was going to bring in enough academic work for my current firm, keep my job, be the sole financial and healthcare benefits provider, *and* simultaneously break into an entirely new market. I didn't want Chris to know that I was stressed, so I kept it inside. I didn't share it with a single person. I didn't want anyone to think I couldn't do it. I didn't want anyone to know that I had doubts about myself.

Chris incorporated his firm in the middle of May 2010. By July the stress had begun to seep into every part of my body and mind. Like I mentioned, the unemployment rate for architects at this time was hovering somewhere around 55 percent, and I worked at one of the largest architecture firms in Boston. As their director of business development, I was responsible for bringing in new academic architecture and planning leads and converting them into business. If I didn't bring in new projects, additional people would most likely be laid off, me included. Having lost millions in endowment due to the stock market crash, most of the college and universities immediately put a freeze on all planned architecture and construction projects.

I woke up one mid-July morning with a terrible case of laryngitis. I essentially speak to other humans for a living, so this was less than ideal. It was further compounded by the fact that I was leaving that day for a three-day conference, which would obviously be filled with networking events and client dinners where I was really going to need my voice.

Three weeks later the situation had only gotten worse. I could barely eke a word out. Chris called the doctor for me because I couldn't speak. He told her the situation and she made an appointment for me to see an ear, nose, and throat specialist that same day. At the ENT's office they fished a camera up my nose and down my throat to get a look-see at what was going on. The doctor removed the camera, looked me straight in the eye, and said, "We need to discuss your stress level." At those words, I began to cry. Straight up sob. Up until that point I wouldn't allow myself to admit that I was stressed, when in reality, I was beyond stressed. The doctor explained that due to stress, acid from my stomach had begun to flow back up my esophagus and irritate my larynx. He explained that I had "very unhealthy vocal chords" because of this.

My treatment was varied: no alcohol, no peppermint, no chocolate, no spicy foods, limited talking, prescription acid reducers twice a day, oh and I needed to see someone about how to reduce my stress levels, and that person had to be a professional.

How could this be? Me, the girl who overcame every obstacle put in my way, and let me tell you there had been a lot of obstacles, both physical and emotional. How the hell was this the thing that broke me? Why could I handle the stress of every other shitty situation up until this point? It wasn't like Chris' firm was struggling. My network had already delivered for him. He was already busy.

I didn't know the answer at that point. I think I probably figured it out in therapy. Therapy isn't easy for a person like me. I ended up firing my therapist because I thought she was too easy on me. I thought I didn't need to pay a professional to tell me that my childhood was difficult. I already knew that. What I thought I needed was someone to look me in the eye and tell me that life is tough and to put on my big girl pants, quit my bitchin', and *chop, chop, off you go.*

But before I pulled the plug, I got a lot of amazing things out of therapy. I learned new ways to cope with stress. I began to understand that you don't have to go 100 miles an hour all of the time, and that there is a grey zone that can exist between the black and the white. The most powerful thing it showed me was that there is power in being heard—to have someone listen to you. If you go to therapy, for one hour a week, you can talk and someone will listen, not just listen but listen and really try to understand. That is powerful. Everyone deserves to be heard. It doesn't mean you're going to like what they have to say about what you've said, but at least you've said it.

Brené Brown in her years of research on shame and vulnerability uncovered that vulnerability is actually the birthplace of love, belonging, joy, and empathy, which we have already talked so much about in this book. She writes, "Vulnerability is about showing up and being seen. It's tough to do that when we're terrified about what people might see or think." And that's what I was—terrified about what people might see or think about me. That fear is what caused my stress, my esophagus to start rebelling, and my vocal chords to fry.

I don't call it a nervous breakdown; I call it a stress-induced health episode. After the episode I knew that I needed to begin to let people know that I was indeed stressed, that I was nervous about Chris' new firm, and that I felt enormous pressure. I had to speak up and be seen. I could no longer hide behind my wide smile and raucous laughter. I needed to start letting people know how I felt. I needed to be more vulnerable, to share more, to be more open about what was happening.

I mentioned at a lunch meeting with a gentleman, who was relatively new to my network but whom I had been helping create relationships within the academic market, that my husband had started a new residential architecture firm. I also mentioned that I felt a little (ha, little) stressed about the fact that in addition to my full-time job, every night and weekend I was working to build his business as well. I explained why my voice was all but absent.

He asked me what he could do to help. He also mentioned that I had already helped him so much, he would be happy to return the favor. Not knowing what he could do besides refer my husband (a man he'd never even met) to anyone who might ask him for a recommendation for an architect (whenever that might be), I gave him Chris' card.

Do you know where this is going?

Two days later Chris received a call from a woman. She had gotten his name from the friend I had lunch with a couple days before. She mentioned that Chris came highly recommended by my friend and that she wanted to meet to discuss a renovation and addition to her house.

Here's what happened: She hired Chris to renovate her house, but halfway through the design process decided she wanted Chris to renovate her beach house first. The house was massive, and right on the water on a beach in Cape Cod. The finished product was stunning. It actually made the cover of a magazine. The neighbors down the street called my husband, asking him to renovate their house as well. Then another one down the street, and more projects after that, until in 2016 my husband was named the Next Wave Architect for the Cape and the Islands.

It would be enough if it ended there, but it doesn't. Chris went on to renovate that initial client's original home, the one he started working on first, and then her daughter's home too. My friend continued to recommend Chris to people he knew. I don't have a grand total, but suffice to say Chris did millions of dollars worth of work resulting from that one lunch I had. One lunch, where I decided to show up and be seen. Where I was strong and vulnerable at the same time.

Honestly, if I can do it, so can you.

CHAPTER 7 TO-DOS: DISCOVER YOUR EQ

1. Go online and take a free EQ test.
2. Implement the "3 Silver Bullets for Increased IQ" at least 3-4 nights per week.
3. Pick at least one "Increasing EQ Exercises" to try.

CHAPTER **8**

NURTURING YOUR RELATIONSHIPS

Many people who teach other people how to build relationships talk about relationships as if they are a ladder. And in order to achieve relationship ROI you need to move the relationship up the rungs of the ladder to the top. I'm not a big fan of ladders. I'm actually a tad bit afraid of heights so I don't want to climb up any ladder. I think if you look at relationships like a ladder you can forget that each relationship has a life of its own and needs to be nurtured in its own unique way. It's not a one-size-fits-all direction to the top.

I recently went to a creative writing retreat to learn and immerse myself in something called Gateless Writing; 'gateless' meaning that it's a way of getting around the internal gatekeeper we all have that tries to tell us our ideas suck and why are we even trying, so that we can write more freely. Remember how I told you that my inner voice is a real asshole? Well, I needed to crash through some gates.

I decided to attend this retreat as I had been struggling to find a more creative way of describing how I feel about networking. At the retreat I began to think about relationship building like tending to a garden. You see, every year at the

129

end of April I begin to lay out my vegetable garden. I turn over the soil in each bed, fertilize the soil with organic matter, and plant my seeds. Each plant takes a different length of time to bear its fruits or vegetables. Some plants as quick as 30 days, some as long as 100 or more. I treat each of these plants with the same exact care: water, sunlight, and pruning. I have to respect the time it takes for each one to grow. Each will bear fruit in its own time; they cannot be rushed. But come September most of those tiny little seeds that I placed in the soil months before will produce a harvest.

So I want you to think about your role in tending to your network and nurturing your relationships in the following stages.

PLANTING SEEDS

This is what we covered in Chapter 3; it includes your pre-meeting research (if you have the opportunity to do so) and your initial meeting. This is where you establish common ground, ask great questions to learn more about the other person, and determine proper and helpful ways to follow up. In my garden, the seeds for each type of plant have certain instructions—how much sun they need, how far apart each seed needs to be so that its growth isn't crowded by others, how much water it needs. During this initial phase of your relationships, learn as much as you can about the other person: how they like to communicate (email, phone, text), and how you can be of help to them. Give your relationship the foundation and environment it needs to thrive.

GROWTH

Once a seed emerges above ground, it doesn't just grow up, it also grows down; the root system below gets stronger, anchoring the plant firmly to the earth and making sure it has access to all the nutrients and water it needs. Similarly, relationships are anchored because you display integrity and trust. This means that whenever you reconnect, you do so with purpose and remember your common ground.

By this point you are investing in the relationship and using their time purposefully. When you reach back out it's with information that might be helpful to them; you ask if you can offer help with anything that they might need, or send them an article that might be interesting to them, or invite them to an event that they would find interesting, or simply let them know you are there should they need anything. When you ask enough questions and really listen to the answers it will be easy for you to begin to understand your potential client's/connection's interests and pain points and how you might be able to provide information that can be of use to them. Each week I get invited or receive information about a number of events, whether it be panel discussions, presentations, or industry networking events. With each invitation, regardless of if I can attend or not, I think about who in my network might benefit from attending. Then I share the information with them. This small act serves to let the people in my network know that I understand what interests them and that I am thinking about them. Just today I received an email from a gentleman in my network, sharing an article titled "The Art of Conversation" with a quick note that said:

J,

I thought you might find this interesting.

R

That's all, just an interesting article on a topic I am passionate about, to let me know that he was thinking of me and understands what I am interested in. The amount of time

132 • JULIE BROWN

it takes for you to do something like this is minimal, but it makes the other person feel special and helps to continue to build that bond between the two of you. It also helps you build what studies have found to be the number one characteristic of the most effective teams: trust. This goes not just for large teams, but for one-to-one relationships as well.

As a business development professional, one of the primary reasons I am so successful is that people can trust me with information. If a consultant gives me a lead about the possibility of an upcoming project on a college campus, or with a major company, or anywhere for that matter, they do so with complete confidence that I will not share that information with their competitors, or with *anyone* who might share it with their competitors. Their leads are kept confidential until the time they say I can share them. Showing this kind of integrity and patience builds a bond with the other person. That person then knows that they can share confidential business information with you.

Some plants flower within days, while others take months or even years. You cannot rush getting to this stage. But you can ensure that you get there by continuing to contribute to the relationship by offering help or assistance. You continue to invest in the relationship before you ask that relationship to benefit you.

PRODUCING FRUIT

This is the point where you can reap the time and effort we have put into the relationship and harvest the fruits of your labor. When you are here, you can freely ask for help, guidance, information, an introduction, or whatever your need is. You get to this point because you have worked hard to nurture and foster that relationship. You ensured that the plant had what it needed to grow and to flourish. Our relationships aren't really plants, so, without a juicy plum hanging from a limb, how do we know that we've reached this stage? I'm not going to quote Van Halen and say, "*It's just something you feel together.*" But it kinda is. You have to be a good judge as to how well you have nurtured this relationship. Have you added value? Do you feel that you are a professional peer? Have you established know, like, and trust? If the answer to those three questions is yes, then I think you've got your plum.

VOLUNTEER CROP

In gardening, there is a term called the 'volunteer crop.' It is essentially a crop you didn't plant. Each year I have volunteer tomatoes, zinnias, snapdragons, peppers, and many more that are a gift from the plants that grew the year before. When your relationships are strong enough to bear fruit, they are also strong enough to provide new referrals and new plants to be tended to, and to do it year after year.

You may be saying to yourself, *I don't have time for all those steps.* Well then, put this book down and continue having mediocre relationships and "meh" levels of success. The day you plant the seed is not the day you eat the fruit. This shit takes time, and if you don't have the patience or the willingness to do the work, you won't succeed. Success is a marathon, not a sprint. You have to have respect for the time it takes to build relationships and get to know, like, and trust.

I'm not the only one saying this. Research shows that 81 percent of deals happen after your fifth contact with a potential client. Coincidentally, this is right around the time that most people give up–especially the douchey, what's-in-it-for-me, not-interested-in-building-real-relationships people. This is what happens when you keep score. I know, it's tempting, but you cannot go tit for tat in a relationship and say things like,

"I emailed them twice, I took them out for lunch, I played 18 holes with them and I haven't gotten shit, screw them."

If this is your mindset, the reason you haven't gotten shit out of your relationships is because you don't deserve it. You aren't authentically building this relationship, you are just phoning it in while waiting for your payday, and then you likely quit before the real decision process even gets started.

I mean, of course, you are building relationships in the hope of gaining more clients. But if all you do is keep score and stop reaching out to people who don't immediately buy from you or help you out in some other way, you will never get to work with 81 percent of your potential clients because you've already given up on them.

A full 89 percent of Forbes 500 company executives say that their relationships have an effect on their business. But only 24 percent of companies have a plan for building business relationships.

Why? Why don't we prioritize relationship building? Because most of us have a relational superiority complex—a belief that our relationships are better and stronger than they actually are.

If only 24 percent of companies have a plan for building relationships, and you create a relationship plan for yourself, you will be ahead of 76 percent of your competition. Seriously, start thinking about creating a plan to build your relationships, grow your garden, and create volunteer crops year after year.

If the plant analogy was too out there for you, here are some ideas for building your relationships based on EQ and IQ.

THIS SH!T WORKS • 135

HOW TO BUILD RELATIONSHIPS VIA EQ

1. **Don't Come Off As Pushy (or Desperate)**

   I don't think this needs an explanation, but if you need one here goes. I'm going to quote serial entrepreneur and author of multiple *New York Times*-bestselling books Gary Vaynerchuk for this. "Don't go for the 19-year-old dude move and try to close on your first transaction. Establish a connection with clients before selling them, offer them a valuable service and then roll deep." Moving in for the sale too quickly makes you look pushy and insensitive.

2. **Be Authentic, Genuine, and Worthy of Belief**

   People can smell bullshit a mile away and if you think they can't you're only fooling yourself. Be authentic when you meet people, have a curiosity for them, learn about them, their job, and how you could help them. When you are asked a question and you don't know the answer, instead of putting together a bullshit answer, say, "That's a great question, let me get back to you on that." And then actually do the work to find the answer and get back to them. Keeping your promises is a big part of building a relationship.

3. **Be a Good Listener**

   Stephen Covey, author of *The Seven Habits of Highly Effective People*, said, "Most people do not listen with the intent to understand; they listen with the intent to reply." It's an old saying, but it rings true. You have two ears and one mouth, use them in that proportion. The more you listen, the more people will talk and share, and the more you can understand how you can help them.

4. **Be Empathetic**

    Empathy isn't hugs and surface-level interactions, it's about putting yourself in someone else's shoes; understanding your client's workload, pressures, and deadlines; your friend's needs, struggle, and personal situation. It's the act of removing your needs from the situation to fully understand the position that someone else is in.

5. **Be Helpful**

    Ask, "How can I help?" Offer information that will be useful; share articles, books or podcasts/interviews that are relevant to that person. Be a source of information or connection. If you have promised to do something for the other person do it. You are judged on your behavior, not your intentions. We all have good intentions; those who act on and follow through on those intentions get noticed.

HOW TO BUILD RELATIONSHIPS VIA IQ

1. **Know Your Shit**

    Listen, we talked about this; All things being equal, people will do business with and refer business to people they know, like, and trust. Well if you don't know your shit then all things aren't equal are they? The first thing you can do to build relationships is to be competent. To take it to another level, do the work to become a thought leader—write articles, participate in panel discussions, and do the work to be an authority on your area of expertise. If you don't know your area of expertise, figure it out. Ask colleagues and friends to help you understand what you know and do that most people don't. Your expertise is closely tied to your point of view—what are you passionate about? What do you perceive that most people are thinking about or doing wrong? Answering these questions will help you uncover your expertise. Lean into it!

2. **Take Detailed Notes**

How are you going to remember everything you talked about with someone, discussed at a meeting, or heard at a panel discussion if you do not write that shit down?

Knowledge is power, and it's a proven fact the brain retains more information when you write it down. When listening to thought leaders write down key points for you to go back to, to inspire yourself. You will not forget what people share with you if you write it down.

If you meet someone at a networking event, take the time to write on the back of their business card the date, the event, and a few of the things you discussed.

When in a face-to-face meeting take notes about what you talk about, write down what you say you will help them with, and what your follow-up tasks are.

3. **Follow Up Consistently**

Keith Ferrazzi, whom I mentioned in the Introduction, says that 80 percent of building and maintaining relationships is just staying in touch. You have to have a plan to follow up with all of the people in your network on a regular basis.

Have your CRM send you an alert, or create a calendar reminder, that nudges you to reach out to three people in your network every week. You can just say hi, share a little info, or ask about something relevant. Most people are terrible at following up; The ones who are good at it stand out and have strong networks that help them achieve a high level of success.

4. **Share Relevant and Interesting Articles**
With the information you uncovered through your dopamine-inducing conversations, you will have discovered what is important and relevant in the lives of your contacts. Take the time to research something that might be interesting to them either on a personal or work basis. Ask them to attend an event with you that has a speaker that would be interesting to them. Offer to tour them through one of your projects, or share a recent win with them.

5. **Follow and Interact with Their Online Presence**
Use LinkedIn, Twitter, Instagram, and Facebook to interact with your contacts online. Liking or even commenting on someone's photo or update keeps you in their awareness. If you want to use the electronic world for deeper interactions, send them a direct message with some thoughts about their recent post. Or, if they send you a newsletter, actually read it and send them an email back with your thoughts. I regularly email my network (and email list) whether it's my bi-monthly ProTip video, thoughts on current events, holiday tidings, or a newsletter. If a person takes the time to respond with their thoughts I always email back to thank them, answer any questions

they may have asked, or simply acknowledge their thoughts.

Now, go back to Chapter 1 and look at your circles of contacts. With each person you listed determine what stage of growth they are in and make a plan to steadily advance that based on what you now know about building relationships with EQ and IQ. Soon you will have plenty of opportunities to be thankful for the folks in your network, which is where gratitude, the subject of the next chapter, comes in.

CHAPTER 8 TO-DOS:
TEND TO YOUR GARDEN

1. Think about the stages of your relationships with each of the people in your circles, and about how you can tend to them all.

2. Make a calendar appointment to reach out to three people in your network each week to reconnect in a thoughtful way.

3. Share an interesting article, book, or paper with two people in your network every week.

CHAPTER 9

A WORD OR TWO ABOUT GRATITUDE AND THE POWER OF THE HANDWRITTEN NOTE

"Gratitude and opportunity create more of the same."

—Seth Godin

By this point in the book you have the tools to create opportunities for yourself. I know that if you network authentically and foster your relationships with a combination of EQ and IQ that opportunities will abound for you. The final thing you need is an attitude that fuels all the tools, tips, and strategies you've learned thus far.

That attitude is being grateful for the people in your network and the relationships that you have.

I hope by now you're clear on the simple truth that no one succeeds alone. Your success depends on a number of people, people who believe in your capabilities and will help you succeed. Having those people in your life is something to be thankful for, dontcha think?

Showing gratitude doesn't have to mean grand, sweeping gestures. It's the small acts of kindness that convey the most gratitude. In fact, I've got a particular action that I want you to start doing regularly that will enrich your life and the lives of the people you're connected to.

Don't worry, I'm not going to ask you to keep a gratitude journal—that activity and its benefits has been heralded from enough rooftops that you've probably gotten this advice at least 100 other times.

Plus, I don't want you to capture what you are grateful for in a notebook and keep it on your bedside table so that only you reap the benefits of this practice. I want you to share your gratitude by giving thanks to those in your network on a consistent basis.

More specifically, I'm asking—no, commanding—you to start sending at least one thank-you card to someone in your network every week.

After all, if you aren't living a life in which you are grateful for at least one person a week, there's something wrong.

Actually writing and then sending the card helps you express how much you appreciate the people in your network instead of just thinking it to yourself. It's how you bridge the gap between intention and action.

HERE IS WHERE YOU START

First, go to the post office and buy a couple sheets of stamps. Please don't get the standard flag stamps; pick some that reflect your personality. I always pick stamps with dogs on them, or national parks, or commemorating someone I look up to.

Then, go to Amazon, Papyrus, or Etsy and choose thank-you cards that—you guessed it—reflect your personality. I have lots of different designs but one of my favorites has a white dog playing a red electric guitar with the text "You

Rock" on the front. The inside is blank so I can write whatever I want about why they rock so much!

Then, once a week, send a thank-you note to someone in your network. This should be easy. What I do is every Friday I look back at the networking meetings that I had during the week, and I send a thank-you card to each person who took time out of their busy schedule to spend time with me. You should be having at least one face-to-face networking opportunity every week, so it shouldn't be a stretch to find one person to mail a card to.

Yes, you have to actually send a card in the old-fashioned mail! I know emailing is faster, but it just doesn't cut the mustard, and here's a major reason why: Only 11 percent of emails are opened, but 100 percent of thank-you cards that are delivered are opened. Not only are they opened, but they are often displayed on the recipient's desk for an extended period of time. I've had numerous people tell me that my thank-you card hung in their office for months. I can promise you, there are no emails printed out and prominently displayed in anyone's office; they may be convenient, but they will never be a visual reminder that you care.

EXAMPLES OF THANK YOUS THAT STAND OUT

One day I had a knock on my office door. When I answered it there was a gentleman standing on my doorstep with a basket of amazing French wines. I hadn't ordered any French wines. He asked if I was Julie Brown. I said that I was. He said, "This is for you." I took the basket and placed it on my desk. I opened the card tucked between the bottles to find a note from a gentleman in my network. He had sent the bottles as a thank you for introducing him to another person in my network, an act that had subsequently led to two projects for him.

I didn't know that my introduction had led to him getting work, and without this amazing gift and note I never would have.

He ended the note by saying, "Thank you for all you do for the people in your network."

My heart was full. Not just because I love wine, but because he had acknowledged what I want most out of networking—helping people connect with others to enrich not just their businesses, but also their lives.

Another day I received a package in the mail filled with cookies and other assorted goodies. Anyone who knows me knows that I also have a killer sweet tooth. When I opened the card it was from a builder I work with; she sent me the gift as a thank you for introducing her to an architect who had chosen her as the builder for two of her projects. Again, I would not have known that my introduction had led to them working together without this thoughtful gift.

Please don't think that you have to send gifts, because you do not. A well-crafted thank-you card is all you need to do. All you have to do is something simple like this.

D -

Thank you so much for your referral to the organizers of the XYZ conference. I am so pleased to be given the opportunity to submit my qualifications as your keynote speaker. Your vote of confidence means the world to me, and I am excited about the possibility of working together to make this a great event for your members.

Cheers,

JB

Or

> J -
>
> *Thank you so much for your introduction to [insert name here].*
> *I recently met her for coffee and we clicked right away. You cer-*
> *tainly have a knack for connecting the right people. If there is*
> *anything I can do for you please do not hesitate to ask. I'd love*
> *to be able to return the favor.*
> *Cheers,*
> *JB*

And

> M -
>
> *Thank you so much for taking the time out of your schedule to*
> *get together for coffee. I know how busy you are and I appreci-*
> *ate you taking a moment to talk with me. I enjoyed learning*
> *about you and your company and I look forward to the possibil-*
> *ity of collaborating together in the future.*
> *Cheers,*
> *JB*

Thank-you notes aren't the only notes you are allowed to send. Handwritten notes of any kind are so powerful, so start sending notes of all kinds.

For example you can and should send a note to congratulate someone in your network on a promotion, award, or major milestone.

On the next page is a note that I sent to a person in my network who was recently promoted to president of his firm.

S-

Just a quick note to congratulate you on your promotion to president. I know how much you have given to your company and this could not have happened to a more deserving or special person.

Best of luck for the future.

Cheers,

JB

There are times when sending an email or commenting on LinkedIn, Facebook, or any other online platform just isn't enough. In fact, it's phoning it in.

I happen to be Facebook friends with a number of my network connections—not all of them, but some of them I am—and I enjoy seeing more of their lives than I might see simply through networking events.

I noticed while scrolling through Facebook that one of my contacts had listed an obituary for his mother. I wanted to try and attend the wake, but it was in another state so I wasn't able to go. I knew that simply commenting on his post wasn't going to convey how I felt, so I took a blank card from my stock of stationary and wrote a letter to him to let him know how sorry I was to hear of the passing of his mother. Losing a parent at any age, for any reason, is difficult, and I wanted him to know I was thinking of him.

A few months later I saw him at a golf tournament that we were both participating in. He pulled me aside to let me know how grateful he was that I had taken the time to send him a letter with my condolences. He said that out of all the people in his network (and he's the president of an architecture firm, so it's a pretty damn big network), I was the only person who took the time to write him a sympathy note, and a handwritten one at that.

I was floored. Are we all so busy that we can't take five minutes to write a note to someone who just lost a parent?

This is why I have the kind of network that is always looking out for me, and that really wants to see me succeed. Because of little things like this, that I do everyday.

You can do these little things too, and I guarantee when you start doing them you will leave your competition behind you.

As I write this chapter, we are four days away from Christmas. Christmas is a special time of year: People are more generous and caring, more willing to help their fellow man. I think back to the scene from A Christmas Carol, with Scrooge waking up on Christmas morning, his view of the world having changed overnight and exclaiming, "I will honour Christmas in my heart, and try to keep it all the year. I will live in the Past, the Present, and the Future."

Here's the thing about networking: It's an infinite game. There is no end to building relationships. Your network is made up of the people you've met in the past and are still nurturing relationships with; it's the people you are meeting now, and it's the people you have yet to meet.

Networking is not just about getting more work, being selected for more projects, selling more things, or even making more money. It's bigger than that. Yes, you are going to get all of those things, but you will also gain friendships, a support structure, and a feeling of belonging.

You will be able to pick up the phone anytime you need information about something, help with something else, or advice on another thing.

You will be able to walk into most rooms knowing that you are surrounded by people who are invested in your success.

You will develop meaningful relationships with amazing people. It's true! Have you ever met someone and thought to yourself how blessed you are to have that person in your life? That shit happens to me all the time. The most wonderful people want to be friends with me even though I don't always know why or understand what they see in me—the girl with all the problems, who grew up on the wrong side of town, who has a hard time being emotionally intelligent, and who clearly has a mouth like a sailor who has been out to sea too long. It will happen for you too.

And perhaps most fulfilling of all, when you develop a robust network, you will be actively involved in the success of others—and, trust me, *that* is a great feeling.

Those are things to be grateful for, aren't they?

So, get out there and network already!

Wait, don't go yet. I want you to know that I am here for you. I want to be a part of your network. I want you to tell me all about Your List of Awesome Shit, and I want to hear about your networking adventures. I wrote this book for you and I am so grateful that you read it, so don't you dare be a stranger. Please reach out to me on LinkedIn, Instagram, Facebook, or send me an email. I can't wait to meet you.

Cheers,

JB

CHAPTER 9 TO-DOS:
BE THANKFUL

1. Buy a sheet of stamps.
2. Pick out some thank-you cards and blank cards.
3. Write one handwritten card/note per week.
4. Send me your list of awesome shit at julie@juliebrownbd.com.

10 LIES ABOUT NETWORKING

Anytime you need a refresher on why networking is important and how to do it, flip right here to the back of this book and re-read the following 10 lies about networking. They are basically the CliffsNotes version of the whole book.

1. **You're Only Supposed To Talk About Work**

   I think that we have established that the highest dopamine-inducing conversations that you can have while at a networking event have nothing to do with work.

   You are totally allowed to talk about work, but please don't let that be all that you talk about. Remember, you are trying to increase the surface area you have to connect with people. Your conversations are giving you the information you can use to build a relationship on. The more you know about the person, the more commonality you can find, the easier it will be to follow up and foster that relationship over the long term.

149

2. **You Have To Be An Extrovert To Be A Good Networker**

    You do not have to be the life of the party at a networking event in order to have meaningful conversations. True networking means having a series of one-on-one conversations, and introverts are great at those. Besides, being an extrovert does not mean that you are good at fostering relationships.

    Introverts are in general better listeners, which means you listen more than you talk. People love to talk about themselves, and the more you can get a person to talk, the more you can learn about them. After reading this book you have the tools to ask amazing questions. Now just sit back, listen, and decide how you are going to take what you learn and use it to foster that relationship.

3. **Networking Only Happens At Events**

    This book proves that networking can happen anywhere. Organized networking events are a wonderful place to meet new people, and you should definitely attend them as a way to increase your network, but you can effectively network nearly anywhere—on a hiking trail, in a bar, at a conference, in the car on the way to the conference, and even on LinkedIn and in your inbox.

    You can also always ask your existing network to introduce you to people. This is a major avenue for meeting new people and advancing your relationships with them, as it has been proven that if two people have a common connection their bond tends to be stronger because of their shared connection.

4. **All Networking Contacts Are The Same**

   When you look at networking like a garden, it's pretty obvious that your relationships are all at different stages of growth. Knowing what stage you are at or which circle of your network each connection is in will help you create a plan to foster each of those relationships.

5. **You Have To Meet A Ton Of People At Every Event To Make It Worth It**

   I tell all of my clients to walk into each networking event with a goal of meeting just two new people. And by "meeting" I mean "have meaningful conversations that can be continued."

   Why do I keep that goal so small? First, if you enter a room with a doable goal, you are more likely to achieve it. And second, you are officially now in the business of creating lasting relationships. So if you have 10 superficial conversations that don't lead anywhere, that is a waste of time. If you only have two meaningful conversations, you have time to follow up the next morning. If you have 10 surface-level conversations it's going to be hard for you to find a compelling reason to follow up the next day to move the relationships forward.

   If you attend only one networking event a week, and at each of those events you meet two new people and then follow up with them, after a year you will have met and begun to foster 104 new relationships. That's way more valuable than trying to talk to everyone at an event and forgetting most of them, isn't it?

6. **You Will Remember Everything And Know When To Follow Up**

   You need to find a system to organize your connections and the information that you have about them. Whether you choose to use a formal customer relationship management (CRM) platform or an Excel spreadsheet, you need to have a centralized location where you can keep all of the data that you have on your contacts as well as when you are in contact with them and need to follow up with them.

7. **Networking Is About Getting Something Fast**

   We've talked about how long it takes for clients to decide if they are going to work with you. Don't walk into a networking event (or meeting) and think that you are going to land a new client, project, or job. Networking is a long-haul game, and you have to give in order to receive. So don't keep score; just keep meeting new people and adding value to your relationships, and good things will come your way.

8. **You're Too Busy**

   Chapter 6 is all about learning how to organize your time so that you can schedule networking into your week, every week. So go back and read that chapter again. Building relationships isn't a skill that is nice to have, it's a must-have in today's workplace. You need to schedule networking into your calendar and respect it like any other meeting or deadline. It's non-negotiable. (Plus, look at lie number three again—networking can happen anywhere.)

9. **You Should Attend As Many Networking Events As Possible**

   Ain't nobody got time for that. Don't spin your wheels and waste your time attending events that aren't targeted for you. Do your research in advance and only attend events based on your industry, who you are trying to meet, and what you can learn. A focused approach to deciding which events to attend ensures you don't overload your calendar and get burned out.

10. **You Don't Have Anything To Offer**

I hear this over and over from people who are just starting out in their career. They are afraid to go to networking events because they don't think they have anything to offer the people that they meet. You have no idea what you can offer someone or how you can help them until you get to know them and ask them how you might be able to help them. Don't apologize for where you are in your career. We all started somewhere, and most people remember very clearly what it was like to be just starting out.

THE 7 KEY TRAITS OF SUCCESSFUL NETWORKERS

Relationships are like buildings: They need structure to support and maintain them. One thing I am good at is structure. (Most people with OCD are.) So here are my seven foundational blocks for building your network. You need:

1. A desire to meet people.
2. A genuine curiosity about who other people are, what their stories are, and what you can learn from them.
3. To seek commonality or even differences that can propel your interactions into the future.
4. To reach out and tend to that relationship, helping it grow—you must be willing to take on that responsibility, and not lay it all on the other person.
5. To remain authentic and worthy of their trust through the entire process.
6. To never enter into a relationship with a "give me" attitude or keep score along the way.
7. To be grateful for the relationship.

ACKNOWLEDGEMENTS

Without **Kate Hanley** this book would just be an idea and maybe a few poorly written chapters. I am indebted to her for helping me create and edit this book. Each page she touched is better because of her talents. Thank you to **Julie Smith** who contributed to this book through careful edits and suggestions, and **Joseph Olshan** who let me know that this book sounds just like me. Thank you to **JuLee Brand** for designing a cover that represents the lessons within the pages of this book. To **Tracey Hartford** and **Jackie Falla** not only for being in my Top 5 and pushing me to do better, but for being there for me throughout my career. To **Shannon Smith**, for convincing me to jump off that bridge with her. And a big loud thank you to *everyone* who has come to hear me speak, who believe in my process and encouraged me to "write a book!"

I'm not sure that this is necessary. I mean, if you've gotten this far in the book you pretty much know all there is to know about Julie Brown. Let's see what else I could put here. . .

Julie lives in Massachusetts during the week and Vermont on the weekends. Due to her two dogs she will never again sleep past 6:30 in the morning.

She hates olives and despises cantaloupe (even you must admit that cantaloupe is the scourge of the fruit bowl).

A child of the 80s Julie wanted desperately to grow up to be part of GLOW, The Gorgeous Ladies of Wrestling! As you can see that dream hasn't been realized. She has however accomplished a few other things. Julie is an in-demand keynote speaker, a sought-after networking coach and business development strategist, and the recipient of the 2020 CREW Boston Entrepreneur of the Year award.

Visit her at www.juliebrownbd.com.

Made in the USA
Las Vegas, NV
25 September 2023

78122765R00095